The Generation Myth

The Generation Myth

How to Improve Intergenerational Relationships in the Workplace

Michael J. Urick

BEP BUSINESS EXPERT PRESS

The Generation Myth: How to Improve Intergenerational Relationships in the Workplace

Copyright © Business Expert Press, LLC, 2019.

First published in 2019 by
Business Expert Press, LLC
222 East 46th Street, New York, NY 10017
www.businessexpertpress.com

ISBN-13: 978-1-94999-111-6 (paperback)
ISBN-13: 978-1-94999-112-3 (e-book)

Business Expert Press Human Resource Management and Organizational Behavior Collection

Collection ISSN: 1946-5637 (print)
Collection ISSN: 1946-5645 (electronic)

Cover and interior design by Exeter Premedia Services Private Ltd., Chennai, India

First edition: 2019

10 9 8 7 6 5 4 3 2 1

Printed in the United States of America.

For Lucy. May you and your "generation" (however you define it) live in, experience, and help to create a better world for everyone—one without needless divisions and stereotypes

Abstract

Generational differences have become a popular topic in society and in the workplace. Yet, many of the often assumed characteristics of particular generational groupings are actually "myths," meaning that generational stereotypes are not accurate across all members of a generation all of the time. This book explores the *Generation Myth* by highlighting the complexity of the "generation" concept beyond simple age-based groupings. Furthermore, a variety of different ways of defining generation (which could be nuanced for each individual) is presented. A major point of this book, however, is to suggest that the overreliance of age-based stereotypes in workplaces and society can lead to less than optimal interactions and even conflict. This book explores how such intergenerational challenges occur in workplaces and suggests several effective strategies for improving intergenerational relationships. The book concludes with suggestions for considering other types of non-generational diversity as well as examining whether or not the strategies useful in a work context can be leveraged in broader society as well.

Keywords

Workplace interactions; generational differences; conflict management; stereotypes; social identity theory; Millennials; Baby Boomers; Generation X; diversity; organizational culture

Contents

Foreword

Every day, we experience interpersonal interactions that are positive, and some that are challenging at best. The role we play when these interactions occur has a significant impact in influencing their outcome. When I consider my own self, in the professional world, I am the CIO for a global manufacturing company and a part-time adjunct professor teaching a graduate level course at a local college. In my personal world, I am a son, a brother, a husband, a father, a grandfather, and a friend. In both scenarios, there are interactions that are easy, smooth, and effortless; conversely, there are other interactions that are contentious, negative, and emotionally draining. Quite frankly, the latter are the encounters I consciously try to avoid. What causes these extreme variances from one interaction to another? A knee-jerk response to that question is to blame the "the generation gap"; but how can this be the reason, since good and bad interactions occur with individuals of all ages and in both professional and personal capacities?

In this book, Dr. Michael Urick explains that perhaps peoples' misconceptions in understanding the term "generation" may cause "problems at work (and in society) including breakdowns in communication, weakened knowledge transfer, and poor intergenerational mentorship." As Dr. Urick outlines, there are many ways of understanding the term generation beyond a simple conceptualization of an age group. For example, a generation can refer to a collective consciousness in which "members of a group have had similar experiences and perspectives because they were exposed to common events, despite potentially possessing different biological ages." In these situations, "generational members emerge because they experience a similar major milestone or life event at the same time despite biological age."

Several years ago, I had the opportunity to meet Dr. Urick, who is the Graduate Director of the Master of Science in Management: Operational Excellence program at the Alex G. McKenna School of Business, Economics, and Government at St. Vincent College in Latrobe,

Pennsylvania. At that time, many manufacturing companies were in the early stages of comprehending the inevitable disruption that would result from Industry 4.0 and digital transformation. My employer was no exception, as experts were predicting that no business, no industry, and even no corner of the world would be spared from the oncoming disruption. Intuitively, to help my company successfully navigate these disruptive changes, I needed to refresh my understanding of the fundamentals of operational excellence (OE), including a focus on optimizing business processes before applying technology. During my first meeting with Dr. Urick, I was quickly convinced that enrolling in the Masters in Operational Excellence program at St. Vincent College would be a benefit on this journey.

In addition to leading the OE program at St. Vincent College, Dr. Urick is also an Associate Professor of Management and Operational Excellence. As an esteemed professor and frequently published researcher, the courses he teaches in the OE program include "Communication, Conflict, and Diversity," "Organizational Culture," and "Organizational Behavior and Human Resource Management." At first, I was dreading the human resources content one anticipates in classes where "organizational" appears in the course title. After all, I had signed up to rekindle my relationship with hardcore OE, like manufacturing type stuff, and not the softer HR content.

Even though my initial strategy was to refresh my knowledge of operational excellence, Lean principles, and the Toyota Production System, I soon found myself completely absorbed in the organizational and human elements of the workplace. Captivated, I found myself mentally revisiting and questioning the way I handled numerous interpersonal interactions during my career. How could this happen? After all, I was thirty-plus years into my career in corporate America. I successfully ascended to the C-suite. I was a global leader skilled in comprehending and expertly managing all workplace dustups that came my way! However, weekly class lectures full of vibrant discussion and debate on topics like conflict management, individual behaviors, and generational bias took me deeper into self-reflection. As I revisited earlier situations in my career (and my personal life), I contemplated using methods learned in class that would have resulted in better outcomes.

Additionally, it was during Dr. Urick's classes that I discovered the depth and breadth of his knowledge in all things people: a knowledge gained not only from extensive research on organizational behaviors and generations in the workplace, but also from his own firsthand industry experience prior to becoming a full-time college professor, researcher, and author. One of the class topics that intrigued me was how real or perceived intergenerational misunderstandings and conflicts lead to "less effective organizations, workplaces, and ultimately societies." Realizing that most of us know less about generational differences than we think, lively class debates provided an introspective glimpse that helped me to reexamine how to "improve my interactions with others, reduce misunderstandings and conflict, leading to an enhanced work product and stronger relationships."

In writing *The Generation Myth*, Dr. Urick has successfully documented the spirit of his courses by extensive research to create a playbook that will help others understand the critical importance of exploring and increasing their understanding of generational phenomena. In the book, readers will understand how enhancing this capability is critical in figuring out how to coexist, work, and interact across multiple generations. This is true whether the generations the reader is bridging are based on age, collective consciousness, or maturity. Personally, I believe that this ability to interact across generations is becoming more critical as social media continues to shrink our world and bring us closer together, Baby Boomers are postponing retirement and remaining in the workplace, and emerging technologies are enabling people of all generational groups to take on leadership roles in corporations, startup companies, or other organizations.

Looking back, I am grateful for the experience that I gained from attending Dr. Urick's classes. Now a fervent advocate and practitioner of the course material, I plan to use *The Generation Myth* as a tool to enlighten others. I firmly believe this understanding and clarity has improved interpersonal relationships in both my professional and personal worlds. As the reader, you now have the advantage to acquire the same knowledge from the book as opposed to attending classes for several semesters. I trust that you will also find valuable lessons from this book that will help you improve interpersonal interactions and relationships in both your professional and personal lives.

In closing, as an admirer of Dr. Urick's work, I am honored for this opportunity to share my thoughts on *The Generation Myth*. However, after reading *The Generation Myth*, I did think to myself, "Could I have waited for the book instead of attending all of those graduate classes?" I wonder if that would be a consistent thought across all generational definitions.

—Thomas F. McKee, Jr.
Vice President and Chief Information Officer, Kennametal Inc.
Latrobe, PA
August 23, 2018

Acknowledgments

There are so many people to whom I am greatly indebted. Without them, this book would not even be a possibility.

I would like to thank those individuals who contributed to an interview or filled out a survey to help make my research possible. Members of SCORE and representatives of the Cincinnati Regional Chamber of Commerce were especially helpful and were supportive of some of my early research in this area.

I would also like to thank BEP Editor Dr. Rob Zwettler for his encouragement in developing this book, as well as his assistance in vastly improving it. I also express my thanks to Dr. Robert Sroufe for letting me know about the opportunity for publishing with BEP.

I am extremely indebted to three individuals who have read early drafts of this book and provided suggestions for improvements. First, Sean Lyons, a preeminent generational scholar and research colleague who I greatly respect, offered deep insights into how the arguments presented in this book might be strengthened. Second, Mark Abramovic, a friend and former executive-turned-professor who has both a managerial and academic background (as well as a great interest in intergenerational phenomena in the workplace), offered some excellent recommendations on how to clarify my statements to an audience of business practitioners. Third, Mary Van Tyne was instrumental in triple checking my grammar, assisting with the formatting of my initial manuscript, and helping to tighten up my writing.

I've also had the pleasure of working with many skilled researchers and coauthors on dozens of collaborations related to intergenerational phenomena. Those that I have not thanked elsewhere in my acknowledgments include Gail Fairhurst, Jim Weber, Therese Sprinkle, Jim Baehr, Lisa Kuron, Linda Schweitzer, and Emma Parry.

I have been blessed with five exceptional mentors who have helped guide my growth and development throughout my career. Dean Gary Quinlivan at Saint Vincent College had faith in me as a new hire into the business department and has given me a great deal of freedom to research and publish on topics of interest to me. Bill Hisker taught the first Organizational Behavior class I ever had and has since become a close friend, colleague, sounding board, and spiritual advisor. When I was a nervous new graduate student, Jay Liebowitz was the first professor who encouraged me to pursue my goals. Elaine Hollensbe was my advisor during my doctoral program and apprenticed me as I developed my research interests on intergenerational phenomena. Suzanne Masterson was the head of my doctoral program who took a chance in accepting me, and also encouraged me as I launched my research program on generations in the workforce.

I also want to acknowledge the faculty and support staff of the Master of Science in Management: Operational Excellence program whom I have not yet acknowledged and who indulge me on my quest to learn more about intergenerational phenomena, including Matt Miller, David Adams, Terrance Smith, Bob Markley, Tom McKee, Pankaj Mehrotra, and Eva Kunkel.

I want to thank my students, particularly those in the MSMOE program, and especially my former graduate assistants Selin Konur and Alperen Arslantas who have worked with me on research.

I would be remiss if I did not include a statement thanking all those from my earlier career as an auditor and training and development manager that got me thinking about generational phenomena, and that influenced me more than they know by leading me down my current career path and research stream.

Finally, and most importantly, I want to thank my family for their unwavering and constant support. I especially want to thank Janet, who helped improve this book with her constructive suggestions, Lucy (who read a very early version of this book), my parents Mickie and Rick, and my grandfather Ug, who first taught me how to read. I know that he would be delighted to see that his grandson has written a book.

Introduction

Let me begin by stating that I don't know if generational differences exist or not, much to the same extent that I don't know for sure that Bigfoot and the Loch Ness monster exist. In my view, they are potentially all myths. Maybe there is some truth to the myth, but it is likely that any truth might have become exaggerated over time. From what I've seen in popular discourse and compared with my own research, I believe that generational phenomena possess a mythical quality—that is, societal and organizational communication about generations can present half-truths that have been exaggerated.

I've spent the past decade exploring the intergenerational phenomenon in the workplace. This book represents a lot of the findings that I have published over the years. As such, there is not much new information here for those who have read some of my academic work or have seen me present my ideas at a conference or at your own organization. However, this book is intended for business professionals and graduate students in professional degree programs, and not necessarily for academics or professors, who were the primary audience of most of my previous writing on the matter of generations. Thus, for readers new to my research, I hope to present a somewhat different take on age and generations at work than what is typically addressed by mainstream media and popular press publications. My background is in organizational behavior, the study of how people work together and relate to the organizations in which they work, and my focus is on intergenerational phenomena at work (whether "work" is at a for-profit business, nonprofit organization, church, school, government agency, etc.), though it is likely that the statements contained herein have implications for broader society as well.

Though I consider myself to primarily be a researcher and academic, I do a lot of public speaking and some consulting related to intergenerational issues in workplaces. I've also done many interviews on the topic on various podcasts and in other media. Almost every time, I get asked the question: "Are generational differences real?" My response to this question, and to other similar questions, is always the same: I don't know and I actually don't care.

Why don't I know? From the research I've read and conducted, I don't see clear evidence of differences between the age groups you often hear popularized in the media. Furthermore, I will share some evidence in this book that I hope will convince you that we, as a whole, actually "know" (meaning we can support with data and true empirical evidence) less about generations and age-based differences than we think we do based on the way we commonly discuss generational phenomena.

To address the second aspect of my answer, why don't I care? A question that this book explores is: "Do differences really matter, or is it the *perceptions* of differences that matter?" In other words, even if we can't academically support the existence of clear differences between generational groupings in the workplace, many employees *believe* that such differences exist, and they enact these skewed perceptions in their workplace interactions. Maybe age groups aren't that different from each other, but we are made to think that they are by the various discourses to which we are exposed—so much so that they set our expectations to believe that differences exist. Thus, we are biased and often believe that there are differences, despite the uniqueness of each individual and despite the lack of empirical support. In turn, these biases lead us to having interactions that are less than ideal.

My goal of improving intergenerational interactions, rather than focusing on any real or unreal differences that divide us, is my overall driving force for writing this book.

Purpose

I had a varied background prior to becoming a full-time academic. I started my career as an internal auditor when I first saw intergenerational interaction challenges at work though, as a fresh college graduate and someone new to the workforce, I didn't recognize them as such. Upon leaving this role and transitioning into my next role in the area of training and development, I began to see these issues more clearly. When I was working in this field many years ago, I came across some material on "managing generations" that one of our instructors was using. This material focused quite heavily on generational differences. The materials highlighted commonly cited traits of Millennials, such as being lazy, acting entitled, and not showing up to work. The materials also highlighted commonly cited traits of Baby Boomers, including that they didn't want to learn, were overly conservative, and were uneasy with change and using technology. Needless to say, these stereotypes were not phrased in a positive way.

I thought to myself, "No one that I know in these generations really fits either of those descriptions." In my role at the time and in previous roles that I had, I had the chance to work with individuals from a variety of generations—and in my work experiences, I have never seen anyone matching either of these broad stereotypes.

I realized that it wasn't just our instructor that was using these descriptors of generations. They were everywhere: from the local news, to special issues of *Time* and *Newsweek* on the topic of generations, to casual discussions that I'd overhear from friends and family members. If you Google "generational differences" right now, you're likely to see a lot of these stereotypical descriptors pop up. I've set up a "Google Alert" to send me an e-mail at the end of every day of news articles related to "generational differences" and, each evening, Google sends me 10–20 links to look at. The popular board game "Monopoly" even has editions for particular generations, in essence mocking them by using the most negative of the groups' stereotypes.

Posts on social media from acquaintances occasionally highlight generational issues. I'm always perplexed when I read some headlines that they share about how Millennials are seemingly "destroying" everything from how wine is consumed to industries that drive the economy. I get frustrated when I read these articles because they rely so heavily on generational stereotypes.

Research has shown that these stereotypes are not often accurate (Costanza, et al. 2012). However, popular discourse has relied on these and other descriptors to set peoples' perceptions of generations. This is problematic because much of what we think we know about generations from hearing the nightly news or reading popular blogs is incorrect. Yet we use these descriptors to set our expectations of others and bring these expectations with us when we enter into interactions with colleagues of various ages. These expectations bias our interactions so much that they diminish our relationships, which in turn can hurt knowledge transfer and mentorship at work.

As a college professor who studies organizational behavior, I'm concerned that this lack of intergenerational learning will lead to less effective organizations, workplaces, and ultimately societies. Therefore, it is my goal in this book to share what I've learned through the past decade of research on generations in the workplace, and to compare my findings with the pop culture perception of generations. In doing so, I hope to debunk the "generation myth" that generations are vastly different from each other to the extent that it makes it impossible to communicate between them. Instead, I will suggest that pop culture-based perceptions make us perceive that generations are more different than they actually are and that perceptions can influence problematic interactions. I hope to dispel the "generation myth" to ultimately improve intergenerational interactions and create better, more productive workplaces.

History

The first chapter of this book presents a brief history of how generations have been discussed in the past, and I'll emphasize how overarching generational theories could be interpreted for the workplace. This first chapter will draw heavily from the field of sociology and especially on the work of Karl Mannheim. Mannheim was an early theorist who wrote on the topic of generations in the 1920s (though perhaps his most influential work was published posthumously and not until the 1950s).

In his work, Mannheim describes a generation as a group of individuals that possess a common identity arising from their "gestalt," a psychological term that refers to a collection of individual pieces that are different from the sum of their parts and that when, taken together, ultimately form a unifying impression. In doing so, such differences are glossed over and those examining the phenomena are left with one unified image of the whole. However, Mannheim notes significant variability in the individual characteristics of the members of each distinct generation, even though they have similar experiences that stem from being a part of the same time and physical location.

Mannheim's perspective—that individual generational members possess a lot of uniqueness—is something that has not often been emphasized by later generational scholars or by the popular press. Instead, more recent work has largely assumed a near carbon-copy approach to imply that every person within a generational grouping is close to identical. Clearly, modern scholars could benefit from rereading Mannheim's forgotten early work.

Definitions

After discussing the history of what's been said about generations, the second chapter of this book addresses how generations have been defined. There is a striking lack of clarity not only about generational labels, but also about the meaning of the term "generation" itself.

In fact, though the popular press has emphasized a definition of generation as an "age cohort," where generations are defined as being comprised of people all born within the same range of years (and certainly, age is a component of many individuals' concepts of generations), in my research I've found that there are seven different ways in which generations have been understood. Academia is just now beginning to discuss more recent understandings, such as generations as identities (i.e., generational labels used to define self or others), generations as weak concepts (i.e., generational labels have limited use or explanatory power in describing expected behaviors or values), and generations as influenced by a contribution (i.e., a generation is recognized when it makes a clear mark on society or an organization).

An individual's concept of "generation" is most likely unique and nuanced from others' concepts, as people draw upon a combination of understandings in ways that are distinct from others. This clouds the concept and makes discussing generations somewhat difficult.

Aside from this, despite the lack of clarity in the "generation" concept, popular culture has continued to advance the "age group" discourse of the term, which marginalizes the other ways of understanding. This has caused an oversimplification of the concept as well as the promulgation of generational stereotypes, which has vast implications for intergenerational workplace interactions.

Consequences

The third chapter considers the implications of the cloudiness of generational understanding. Since most people have a unique and nuanced understanding of generations, there are potentially an infinite number of ways in which the term "generation" could be interpreted. However, there are also hundreds of popular press publications and corporate training events that seemingly assume that everyone views "generation" as meaning the same thing. This oversimplification of generational phenomena could potentially cause misunderstandings of news that we hear, training we experience, or articles that we read. It could also cause individuals to disengage in discussing generational issues if they don't understand (or agree upon) an interpretation of the term that is being emphasized in the conversation. Nonetheless, it is important to discuss intergenerational phenomena, especially in the workplace, as modern organizations are currently the most age-diverse that they have ever been.

More importantly, many nonacademic (and some academic) discussions of generations focus exclusively on age-based differences and stereotypes. This leads to a lot of biases, such that individuals expect others whom they perceive to be of a particular age to exhibit prototypical characteristics of an often arbitrary (albeit age-based) identity group. These expectations can often be characterized by negative descriptors such as lazy or unchanging, as noted earlier in this introduction. Negative labels and adjectives are bad enough, but the impact that they have on interpersonal interactions is even worse. Having negative images in our minds leads to less fruitful interactions when we are predisposed to think negatively of the person with whom we are communicating. This leads to inefficient and negative workplaces, as well as a reduction in knowledge transfer and mentorship. In turn, since we expect younger employees to soon inherit crucial decision-making and leadership roles as Baby Boomers exit the workplace, a lack of preparation due to breakdowns in communication will make them less effective than our organizations and society will both expect and require.

Furthermore, focusing primarily on differences in our discourse on generations creates a caustic culture, both in our workplaces and in society as a whole. Too often, our conversations emphasize those things that divide us when there are likely equally as many things that could unite us. In today's turbulent times, attempting to unify rather than divide is crucial toward developing a positive culture, both in the workplace and beyond.

Strategies for Improving Interactions

In my and my colleagues' research (Urick, Hollensbe, and Masterson, et al. 2017), we try to put a positive spin on challenging intergenerational interactions, especially as they apply to the workplace. In our work, rather than ignoring generational stereotypes, we identify them explicitly, and advance intergenerational knowledge in a crucial way. Our positive spin is to offer strategies that can be used to improve interactions. I discuss interaction challenges in the fourth chapter but emphasize this positive approach in the fifth chapter.

Most of my academic work related to generations focuses on bringing people of all ages together to facilitate knowledge transfer and mentorship. I summarize some of the findings of my research on how people attempt to improve their intergenerational interactions. I also summarize some interesting findings that show great variation *within* a generation, further cementing the idea that, when engaging in interactions, it's best to get to know the individual with whom you are interacting rather than relying on perceived generational stereotypes.

Broadening the Application

In the conclusion, I speculate whether my findings on intergenerational phenomena can be expanded outside of the workplace to broader society. I also consider the implications of my research on other areas of diversity, such as gender, race, religion, sexual orientation, and other types of identities. In doing so, I hope that this book can positively influence better communication in the workplace and in society for people of all ages, experiences, and walks of life.

Summary

This introduction lays out the roadmap for this book. Throughout *The Generation Myth*, I will explore the following:

- The history of generational studies shows that what we know about generations is complex and nuanced but is often overly simplified in modern accounts.
- There are many ways of understanding the term "generation" beyond a simple age group conceptualization.
- Misunderstanding generational phenomena can lead to problems at work (and in society), including breakdowns in communication, weakened knowledge transfer, and poor intergenerational mentorship.
- Negative consequences of biases of other generations' members can be lessened by engaging in several effective strategies.

I hope that you find the exploration of the "generation myth" presented in this book to be interesting, thought-provoking, and at times challenging.

CHAPTER 1

A History of Uncertainty

When U.S. Senator John McCain passed away in 2018, his one-time political opponent, former president Barack Obama, began a written statement by stating "John McCain and I were members of different generations, came from completely different backgrounds, and competed at the highest level of politics. But we shared, for all our differences, a fidelity to something higher…" (Pennell 2018). This statement illustrates just how pervasive the idea of generational differences has become. President Obama could have opened his statements by listing a number of differences between himself and Senator McCain including, most notably, their differences in political ideology. But, seemingly, their differences in generation were more salient in how President Obama differentiated himself from the late senator. Such a salience possessed by an individual who has held the highest elected office in the United States is mirrored throughout our society.

As an informed society, we presume that we know a lot about generations; yet much of what was known from past theorists has been forgotten. This chapter begins with a reintroduction of how generations were discussed decades ago from a sociological perspective and then suggests that the original complexity of intergenerational phenomena has been overly simplified with time; hence, the need to further examine the "generation myth."

Mannheim's Perspective

Karl Mannheim's work has been extremely influential in the field of sociology (Pilcher 1994). Though many of his influential works were written in the 1920s, most were not widely published until after his death in 1947. According to Mannheim (1970), a generation is an illusion whereby an "identity of location, embracing related 'age groups' in a historical-social process," creates a "gestalt" (Mannheim 1970, p. 382). I take "gestalt" to mean "oneness." Individuals and society might perceive oneness within a generation and believe that the collective characteristics of a generation apply to all individuals who they perceive to be members of a particular grouping. This definition of generation emphasizes a common location in terms of an historic time period, as well as having a collective conscious-ness (whereby generational members share similar understandings and interpretations of the world around them—more on this concept later in this book; Joshi, Dencker, and Franz 2011). However, it also suggests that generations are not strongly defined. In fact, Mannheim refers to them as "illusions," and perhaps this is an acknowledgment of the variations within a generation that are likely to exist.

Other sociologists were influenced by Mannheim's initial concept and support his definition in their research. For instance, sociologist Dr. Jane Pilcher (Pilcher 1994) states that the term "generation" is used for mak-ing sense of the differences that exist between members of various age groupings and, along with professors June Edmunds and Bryan Turner (Edmunds and Turner 2002), notes that cultural change is reflexively created and reinforced through such groupings. From this perspective, thought leaders help to provide a generation with its own unique phi-losophy, which ultimately leads to changes within society as the ideals and philosophies of prior generations lose sway. Such societal changes can thereby reinforce individuals' concepts of themselves as members of a particular generation. In other words, some individuals who identify with a particular thought leader, her or his values, and the cultural shifts seemingly brought about by this person (or persons) are likely to consider themselves to be part of a particular generational group.

However, it is possible that not all people of a same certain age define themselves by the same generational label. Though useful, Edmunds' and Turner's view (Edmunds and Turner 2002), which explains how a concept of generation is reinforced, does not consider whether (or how) some individuals associate with a generation if they disagree with or are unaware of the ideals that are stated by the generation's thought leaders.

Not identifying with a generation makes sense when considering Mannheim's initial theory. Though it is labeled a gestalt and Mannheim suggests that generations possess a collective consciousness, he also alludes to the fact that individuals of particular age groups (i.e., generations) also show great uniqueness. Therefore, individual traits are often overlooked due to the illusion of oneness within a generation.

Oversimplifying "Generation"

The popular discourse on generations serves to conceal the fact that much extant research (at least within the realm of scholarly business research) has not examined generational phenomena under the guidance of a clear and distinct "generation concept." That is, the way that researchers have defined a "generation" has varied over time and between researchers. Though attempts have been made to clarify and better define what the concept of generation represents (see Joshi, Dencker, and Franz 2011 for example [and more on their approach in the next chapter]), most business research falls back on examining the differences between age cohorts in the workplace. Unfortunately, this approach is often taken by popular press publications and common daily conversations that surround the topic of generational phenomena, including President Obama's statement at the beginning of this chapter. It is quite possible, though, that "generation" is a more nuanced and distinct concept, as Mannheim hints. A purely age-based concept is clearly not what he suggests in his references to time *and* location, as well as the *perceptions* of a "gestalt" (i.e., considering the illusion of oneness or sameness) among members of a generation.

Pilcher (1994) states that Mannheim's initial concept has been so overly simplified that the idea of "generation" is now cloudy and ambiguous. When concepts become too simplified, their usefulness diminishes. Cloudiness in generational understandings has significant implications for researchers and, perhaps even more importantly, for both the workplace and society. On the research side, researchers who study "generations" could actually be studying different phenomena, though they may be labeling them similarly. For example, one researcher might use the term "generation" to analyze differences between members of particular age groupings, while another researcher might use the term to describe a group of employees who were hired into an organization at the same time (i.e., a generation of employees to enter an organization), and a third researcher might use the term to describe how people within a family relate to each other (i.e., lineage). All of these potential meanings of "generation" are noted by organizational researcher Aparna Joshi and her colleagues (Joshi, Dencker, and Franz 2011; Joshi, Dencker, et al. 2017) and have been leveraged by scholarly researchers (albeit some more than others), but only the first (i.e., a strictly age-based approach) has been, as of yet, widely used in the popular press.

This approach is problematic because the ultimate role of academic research is to inform the public about important phenomena from a scientific perspective. If academics cannot agree on, or at least clearly specify, what a generation is, it is unlikely that public knowledge (which should be influenced by academic research) will also have a concrete grasp on the concept of "generation." Similarly, if an academic's definition is unique from the common societal understanding of "generation," that person's research results might not be well received by a nonacademic audience.

The cloudiness of the term "generation" is problematic, not just for researchers and academics, but also for business people in the workplace and for society as a whole. Employees who must attend training related to generational differences might not have the same understanding of a generation as fellow participants. In a sense, this could lead to training attendees speaking a different language from the training facilitator. The same issue might occur when individuals read publications on generations without the same definition as the one that the author assumes. In both cases, having a number of competing meanings for the term "generation" weakens the usefulness of the term and the phenomena that it represents. Even more troubling, the overuse of differences and stereotypes to describe somewhat arbitrary age-based groupings to discuss generations (as has been done often in popular discourse) can create an abundance of problems. Some of these problems are discussed in the next section and later in this book.

Use in the Discourse of Popular Culture

The term "generational differences" has become buzzworthy within the United States and throughout the world, as interest at a superficial level on generational phenomena has seemingly continued to rise. Improving the quality of intergenerational interactions at work is so important that many organizations feel the need to offer employee training in this area (Society for Human Resource Management 2005). Many practitioner-oriented publications have focused on the issues of generations in workplace contexts. One example of an important issue that has arisen is that, as older employees continue to work longer instead of retiring and younger employees join the workforce (and are sometimes expected to quickly assume leadership or decision-making roles), members of various generations need to communicate and function effectively together (Zemke 2001). A quick search through a bookstore or Amazon.com on mainstream popular publications related to generational differences, especially those directed toward working professionals, shows evidence that generational concerns are a significant issue.

When reading through the titles of these books and other articles on generational differences, I'm often struck at how many refer to conflict or views that members of particular generational categories behave problematically in some way. Note that many of them set up an "us versus them" conflict or power struggles to influence us to expect generational differences when we encounter someone from another generation. Some of the most extreme cases include titles that reference "age rage" or note that members of younger generations are "strangers." Most of these titles focus on assumed differences that have not been academically confirmed. In essence, we are spreading lies or half-truths and setting up our culture to assume that intergenerational conflict is inevitable. Some stereotypes that I have heard of, though that are not necessarily "proven" by academia, seem to stress the differences between groupings, as shown in Table 1.1. Note that the purpose of providing such a chart is not to show my own agreement with these descriptors, but to merely show the ways in which generations have been popularly discussed. Also, while I include birth years from the cited references, these may vary depending on if you read a different reference.

How pervasive is the topic of generations in popular discourse? Let me share a personal story as an example. In December 2017, I attended a training seminar that was officially sponsored by a large international professional organization near Washington, DC. It was a three-day session attended by about 40 business professionals, and I was the only professor or academic in attendance. The session was on a topic that was

Table 1.1 Popular stereotypes of generational groupings

Generation label and approximate birth years	Typical descriptors
Veterans/silents/traditionalists/mature (1922–1943)	Respectful of authority; work is an obligation; likes structure; follows rules; respects experience; distrust in technology; nonforward thinking
Baby Boomers (1943–1960)	Focused on career; self-absorbed; unchanging; conservative
Generation X (1960–1980)	Disrespectful of leadership; independent; the forgotten generation; careers are an irritant
Millennials/Generation Y (1980–2000)	Demanding of respect; comfortable with change; technology-focused; creative; entitled
Generation Z/Makers (born after 2000)	Entirely dependent on technology; prefers security and stability; multitaskers; focus on crowd-sourced solutions

Adapted from (QuotesGram n.d.) and (Generational Differences Chart n.d.)

completely unrelated to generational differences in the workplace—and yet, the instructor referred to popular stereotypes of generations that were mostly inaccurate or unsupported by research nearly 120 times (I started counting after an hour into the first day and lost count by the afternoon of the third day)! As the attendees considered this instructor to be an authority, I wonder how many walked away believing his statements about generations. I will note that I shared my research with him following the session in the hope that he would stop leveraging unfounded stereotypes in his sessions.

While popular discourse often focuses on the differences among generations and on both the positive and negative stereotypes associated with specific generations (for example, that Millennials are good with technology or that members of the Baby Boomer generation are likely to have long tenures with their employers), few publications or training events address the nuances of the generation concept that have been previously noted. They also do not address how or why individuals choose to act or not act in a manner that's consistent with a generation's stereotypical expectations. For example, consider those individuals who do not personally fit their generation's stereotypes, yet act in a manner that supports those stereotypes. Imagine a member of a younger generation who is not comfortable with technology but who volunteers for a tech-related task; or a member of an older generation who wants to leave her role for a better opportunity, yet does not do so in part because she's afraid that another organization will ask why she is leaving her current job, since Baby Boomers are assumed to prefer stability in their careers. In both situations, these employees engage in behaviors that might make them personally uncomfortable (e.g., volunteering for a tech role or staying in a job that leads to unhappiness), yet they act in these manners when these actions are supported by expectations that others have of them in a professional context despite not feeling a personal fit with these generational expectations.

Throughout my research, I've noted the following: (1) academic research does not support many of the stereotypical attributes associated with certain generations; (2) the concept of generation is often used to help individuals make sense of perceived differences in age-based groupings; and (3) individuals may come to either identify or dis-identify with the gestalt of perceived generational stereotypes, even those that are not supported by research. In other words, some individuals adjust their behavior to either conform with or distance themselves from stereotypical generational expectations. From this analysis, two questions become apparent:

- Why do individuals enact or adopt generational stereotypes even if they do not fit their personalities, beliefs, or personal values?
- How are generational identities that enact stereotypes encouraged to continue in society, even though research has found them to be inaccurate?

As I note in an article published in the *Journal of Intergenerational Relationships* (Urick 2014), I believe that both of these questions can be informed by the theories of Erving Goffman, one of the most influential sociologists of the last century. In particular, Goffman's dramaturgical theory (Goffman 1959) is useful when considering generations as this theory illustrates why employees might engage in what organizational behavior researchers have termed "impression management" (Bolino, et al. 2008). Using dramaturgical theory can help make sense of why an individual might "act" (by which I mean behave as an actor on a stage does) or perform in a way to make others within a given context think that they either fit or do not fit a generation's (as Mannheim puts it) "illusion" of oneness. When an employee engages in behaviors that fit with a generation's stereotypical expectations—even if they don't personally feel comfortable doing so—this supports the illusion of oneness and allows for generational stereotypes to continue. For example, consider the newly hired member of a younger generation who does not like to leverage technology at work, yet takes on technology-oriented assignments in her workplace. Because she is expected to volunteer for these types of assignments in her work context based on her age, she feels that taking on these roles will help her achieve a positive outcome, such as an eventual promotion. In other words, she "acts" according to the expectations that coworkers perceive are typical of her generation, even though she does not personally feel comfortable engaging in these activities. In doing so, she perpetuates the belief that all members of a younger generation enjoy working with technology. This type of behavior is precisely what Goffman considers.

In *The Presentation of Self in Everyday Life* (Goffman 1959), Goffman explores the roles that individuals perform when engaging in actions. He argues that individuals are "on stage" when they are "acting" out roles in order to fulfill societal expectations. When considering generations, these expectations can form from Mannheim's "illusion" of a gestalt, which creates expectations on how an individual should behave based on their membership in a certain generation.

The theory that the way that a person acts can change depending upon the context or situation has been supported in research on generational phenomena in organizations. Perceived stereotypes of incompetence may lead older workers to resist accepting assignments when they are viewed as challenging (Maurer, et al. 2008), for example. Perhaps unsurprisingly, if a mature worker is expected to fail in an assignment because of the generation that they belong to, they will likely act in a way that supports such societal expectations. By not accepting such an assignment, organizations could be missing out on the knowledge, skills, and abilities that are necessary to complete such a goal. In essence, dramaturgical theory has an impact on organizational performance: the individual will act in a manner so as to more effectively play to an audience. Once the situation is defined, the individual will seek to act in accordance with expectations that will make them appear in a positive manner to others. But how does an actor define the situation? In other words, how do they discover what the expectations might be of their generational role?

Often, one's understanding of generational expectations comes from age-based stereotypes that are commonly discussed in popular discourse. Having an understanding of generational discourse can manifest itself in various behaviors in one of two ways. As previously noted, the first is that individuals might choose to act in accordance with common generational stereotypes when doing so within an organization will produce positive consequences, such as achieving a higher salary, or places them within a social collective within an organization that has power or prestige of some type (known academically as an in-group). The second manifestation is that individuals might choose to act in a manner that distances themselves from generational stereotypes if they perceive that doing so will produce positive consequences in cases where extreme generational biases might exist that limit the potential positive experiences that an individual might have. This is related to the concept of psychosocial age where individuals may seek to act in ways to cause them to be perceived to be either older or younger (Kooij, et al. 2008) in order to fit within a certain context or meet specific stereotypical expectations. The bottom line is that, according to dramaturgical theory, individuals will use their knowledge of generational expectations from how they've already heard generations discussed to adjust their behaviors to achieve positive results.

As such, a key point of Goffman's approach (Goffman 1959) is that individuals act in certain ways in which they see a benefit within a given context. From his approach, one's behaviors are adjusted within her or his context for the purpose of controlling an impression on an audience. In other words, even though an individual might act in accordance with generational stereotypes (supporting Mannheim's illusion of the gestalt) in one situation does not mean that he or she will support these stereotypes in all situations. For example, consider once again the Millennial generational stereotype of technology proficiency. When a member of the

Millennial generation is on a team tasked with rolling out a new software system, this person may seek to act in accordance with the often-positive Millennial stereotype of being good with technology in order to impress upon others that they are members of this generation. After all, doing so could likely lead to positive outcomes for that individual: respect within a multigenerational work group, self and others' confidence in the person's ability to perform, and perhaps workplace advancement opportunities.

Alternately, this same person may seek to act in ways that are dissimilar from Millennial stereotypes, such as having limited work experience, when sitting on an executive leadership team where its members are expected to possess practical decision-making experience. In this situation, a younger employee might arrive early to a meeting, dress more conservatively than might be expected of members of their generation, or shy away from taking notes on an electronic device to distance themselves from Millennial stereotypes. Some stereotypes that this person is actively seeking to avoid could include a lack of concern with deadlines (i.e., perhaps related to laziness or a sense of entitlement), informal preferences in appearance and attitude, and (in this case, perhaps the negative stereotype of) proficiency with technology. By acting in ways dissimilar from these stereotypes, an individual actor is essentially trying to send a signal that they are more mature than how a typical member of the Millennial generation is stereotyped. In essence, by using impression management techniques to either act in a way that supports or does not support membership and oneness with a generation, the individual will choose to draw or not draw on accepted generational stereotypes to give the impression to the audience of belonging or not in order to benefit their goals in a given situation.

What is meant by "context" or "situation?" Although context is a broad term, this partially refers to the generational discourse to which a person is exposed. Such discourse is not only encountered at the societal and interpersonal levels, but also at the organizational level, and thus could be unique for each organization. As a result, it is likely to be heavily influenced by an organization's culture. In a workplace setting, context or situation could include an organization's culture or structure, as well as nuanced aspects of the industry. For example, consider a tech startup in which a majority of employees belong to a younger generation.

Youthfulness, an entrepreneurial and innovation-oriented attitude, and tech-savviness are often assumed to be related to age and valued within a culture of such an organization. For a Baby Boomer who is perceived to not want to change, to be out-of-touch with current technology, and to have an old-fashioned attitude, impression management techniques, including changing one's appearance to look younger, consistently discussing successful tech-oriented roles during an interview, or taking the lead on working on highly technical tasks are ways in which they might "act" in order to fit in within this particular work setting.

As each culture values different things and each industry requires different skills to successfully compete, each workplace context is unique. Certain generations might be perceived to possess or lack the required skills (such as technology proficiency) that are needed to help an organization remain competitive. Some aspects of workplace context might include the following:

- *The importance and acknowledgment of generational categories*: This includes the generations of the audience and other actors, as well as the amount of influence that actors attribute to generation as a gauge of status, knowledge, or expertise; for example, do most organizational members belong to a certain generation that is perceived to possess important skills?
- *The pervasiveness of generational stereotypes and expectations*: Pervasiveness leads to preconceived notions of how generational members will act; for example, does the organization provide "company-approved" training on "generational differences" that reinforces stereotypical (but perhaps not academically supported) generational characteristics?
- *The skills required for job or task completion*: This includes their relationship to the perceived skills that are inherent in generational stereotypes; for example, is innovation important within an organization's industry, and are Millennials perceived to excel at "pushing the envelope" to help develop new products?
- *The strength of other demographic descriptors, roles, and identities of actors*: This may encompass race, ethnicity, gender, family

situation, and work or nonwork roles among others; for example, is belonging to a certain age or generation overshadowed by a common goal of being a contributor to the organization, thereby lessening the negative effects of multiple generations working together?

- *The values of the organization and nation/geographic region*: These may include the need for representation of generational "tokens" for diversity programs; for example, do mature generations feel that they are part of an organization primarily because the organization wants older generational categories to be represented in a workforce solely to fill quotas, and not because they possess needed skills?

- *Personal characteristics of the actors*: This encompasses personality, prior experiences, the knowledge and skill of acting in accordance with stereotypes, one's values, and the personal level of investment in a generational category; for example, have employees regularly interacted with members from other generations, such that they have firsthand evidence that supports (or does not support) generational stereotypes?

Using these aspects of context, organizational actors will analyze their environment and try to manage their impression so that they will receive favorable outcomes, whether for the individual or for the organization. Examples of individual favorable outcomes include raises, promotions, being assigned to prestigious projects, and gaining the respect of coworkers. Examples of organization-wide favorable outcomes include attracting more customers, increasing profits, enticing additional investors, and becoming an attractive workplace for potential employees.

A more detailed hypothetical example is presented here to serve as a further illustration. Consider an employee in a younger generation who was recently hired at a law firm on the basis of her law school grades. However, when she enters the firm, she notices that a majority of the employees belong to an older generation. Furthermore, discussions of generational stereotypes are common. Among these discussions are anecdotes that younger generations do not possess the skills needed to be successful in representing clients because they do not have the same experience or personal network within the legal community as members of older generations. In a typical day, it is not uncommon for this employee to hear jokes about her age. She is consistently passed up for promotions and high-profile assignments (despite outperforming her older colleagues), and she attributes these occurrences to her membership of a particular generation based on her experiences with the organization's culture.

This particular employee does not conform to the biased and stereotypical representation that her coworkers have of her generation (back to Mannheim's "illusion" of its perceived oneness) and feels anger and frustration within her workplace. Like her colleagues, she has the skills needed to be successful and desires to achieve promotions and work on prestigious projects. However, instead of resigning due to this frustration, this employee decides to enact a different generational identity. She may change her physical appearance by changing her hair style, wearing glasses, or dressing more conservatively to make herself seem "older." She consistently discusses her recent court case successes with colleagues from an older generation. Though each of these activities take some level of effort beyond what could be expected of other employees (and beyond what *should* be expected of her), she perceives that all of these new ways of "acting" will help others to not see her as a member of a younger generation, but instead as a solid contributor in the workforce. As a result, she hopes that she will be given the next high-profile assignment.

Introducing the "Generation Myth"

The premise of this book is to suggest that much of what we know about generations, intergenerational interactions, and generational differences is, in fact, not accurate. Thus, I've formulated what I call the "generation myth."

What is a myth? Several years ago, I went to a "Bigfoot convention" with a friend of mine that was full of enthusiasts of the legendary beast. I went because I'm intrigued by this animal and the people who insist that they've had an experience with it. While there, I noted many presenters attempting to share evidence that shows the existence of Bigfoot. As someone skeptical of the existence of Bigfoot, the evidence was not compelling—but to those in attendance who believed that they had encountered the creature, the presenters were convincing. Thus, myths can help affirm what we already believe.

Myths also help us to make sense of the world we encounter. The ancient Greeks believed in the myths of the gods of Mount Olympus to help them understand natural occurrences, including the weather and astral phenomena.

However, myths can also contain an element of truth. My favorite author is J. R. R. Tolkien who wrote many myths. Tolkien believed that all myths had an element of truth if they resonated with the human spirit (Tolkien, Tolkien, and Carpenter 2000). While the specifics and details of each mythical story might not be exact, the spirit of the story contains truth if it resonates with something deep in people's psyche (and, as Tolkien might say, "soul").

From these statements, then, the concept of generation as myth makes sense. Believers in generational categories and differences look for evidence and toss out pieces of data that do not confirm their bias, just as believers of Bigfoot believe in spurious evidence of its existence. Yet, people are drawn to common generational categories because they help us make sense of and create order in our world, just as the ancient Greek myths helped to explain phenomena that they did not understand. On the other hand, examining generations can help us pay attention to potential challenges and difficult workplace interactions, which suggests that there may be some elements of usefulness to exploring generational categories and differences as suggested by Tolkien's perspective on myths.

Furthermore, I define the "generation myth" in much the same way that Mannheim discussed the concept of generation before it was overly simplified to focus primarily on age-based stereotypes, when he referred to it as an "illusion" of oneness. While there may be some similarities between members of a certain age grouping, the idea of clear generational groupings is a myth, because of the following:

1. There is a lack of agreement on the exact years in which generations begin and end. Read a few popular press or even academic articles on the topic and you will see that each likely has different demarcations for when generational groups begin and end.

2. Given that some generational groups have decades-long spans of birth years to indicate membership, those individuals on the cusps of generations are perhaps similar to individuals who may only be a few birth years apart but may be labeled as part of a different generation. They also might not share much in common (in terms of generationally dictated values, ideals, or behaviors) with others who are potentially 20 years older or younger but are also labeled to be part of the individual's generation.

3. Given the above discussion, there are likely many instances in which individuals do not fit well with the assumed characteristics of their birth-year–related generation.

To formally define the "generation myth," I suggest the following:

The elusive connection between birth year, or belonging to a particular generational label, and most of an individual's behaviors or values.

I explore the concept of the generation myth and continue to question the explanatory power that one's generation possesses throughout this book.

Summary

This chapter introduced the idea of the "generation myth" and questioned how much we actually know about generational phenomena. It further addressed the following:

- Classic conceptualizations of "generations" from sociology suggest complexity: They consider a generation to be based on more than just biological age but included "location" and an "illusion" of oneness while suggesting that a great deal of variability can exist between members of a generational group.
- Yet, the complexity of "generations" has largely vanished from popular discourse, which has overly simplified a "generation" to an age-based group.

- This simplification has led to (often negative) perceptions of particular age groups that influence how people act and interact.
- The "generation myth" suggests that we know less about generations than we may think and asks us to reexamine what we know to improve interactions, knowledge transfer, and mentorship.

What does the "generation myth" mean to real-world business professionals? Awareness goes a long way in improving interactions. For business people who are reading this, understanding that generational categories and differences are not necessarily exact or 100 percent accurate can go a long way toward reducing generational biases in the workplace while improving interactions. Thus, it is my hope that we can begin to question what we think we know about generations, so that we can build an approach to interacting with work colleagues that is based more on individuals and less on generational stereotypes.

Improving what we know can become difficult because, as we will see in the next chapter, the definitions and understandings of "generation" and "generational categories" are likely to be different for each individual. The next chapter helps us to explore a myriad of definitions.

CHAPTER 2

Defining "Generation"

Hebrew Scripture tells the story of the Tower of Babel. This story represents a myth about how and why people around the world speak different languages. The story recounts that people (who had all previously communicated using the same language) tried to build a tower so high that it would reach heaven so they could become divine. But, through the process of building the tower, their speech became confounded so that they could not understand each other, and as a result, different languages were created.

The study of generations at work is similar to this myth in that, though one definition of generation has been advanced almost exclusively in popular discourse, there are a number of other ways that the idea of "generation" can be understood. Just as in the story of the Tower of Babel, confusion and misunderstanding can occur when people fail to speak the same language when they discuss generational phenomena. As this chapter will show, it is possible that each individual has a somewhat nuanced understanding of generations, despite the pervasive age-based definition that workforce training events, popular business publications, and everyday conversations rely on constantly.

The previous chapter explored the history of how both researchers and society at large have understood and studied generations. At its conclusion, the chapter highlighted the idea of the "generation myth" that suggests that we actually know less about generations than we think; or, rather, that what is often considered to be accurate knowledge about generations is inaccurate. Perhaps individuals intuitively know quite a lot about generations. However, the way generations are discussed in popular culture is often overly simplified, such that common discourse influences society to think generations are less complex than they actually are (and less complex than our individual instincts tell us that they are). As individuals abandon their own complex views for the adoption of the oversimplified versions that they often hear, more problems are created. Therefore, this chapter explores the complexity of the generation phenomena by suggesting a variety of ways in which "generation" has been understood. It begins by articulating a strictly biological age-based approach, which is the simplest and most common understanding of generation found in popular discourse.

In research that I've worked on with my colleagues, we've identified seven different ways that "generation" can be understood. They are listed in Table 2.1 (and are elaborated in this chapter). The table includes some representative quotes from interviews that we conducted during the course of our research.

Table 2.1 Categories and examples of ways to understand "generation"

Category of understanding	Details	Illustrative quotes
Collective consciousness	**Growth time/environment:** Individuals in generations grow up during a similar time and in a similar place, which helps to set their collective understanding	"I belong to the generation that grew up in the 1940s with the wars and in the 1950s, from an educational point of view, in a small town where everybody knew you."
	Historic events: Members of a generation experience and understand specific historic events similarly during their formative years, which leads to trends within their generation	"Baby Boomers, they had their Woodstock; they had their 'free' period, and now they're focused. I would imagine Baby Boomers are a bit scared because of retirement funds and their savings and things like that [which] are not as stable as they thought they were. So they thought they could retire sooner rather than later and that's not the case."
	Media influence: Members of particular generations are characterized by how they're portrayed in the media, or by types of media that were influential at certain times	"The music of the current generation is basically monochromatic—the same. I define some of it as bang and scream and it's the same notes over and over again and it's the same words over and over again. That's one distinction I make that I see. Another generation I see is my own generation. They perceive the 1950s as the Rock and Roll Generation…Everybody talks about the 1950s being the Elvis era."

Genealogy	Lineage: Generations are defined by lineage within a family or organizational structure (parent-child, third generation born in the US, second CEO)	"It's a simple word: 'generations.' I'm one generation; my parents are another one, and my grandparents were another one, so nothing fancy."
	Placement within context of other generational groups: Generations are defined by their interface with other generations; one knows one's own generation based on the borders of an older and/or younger generation	"Well it means, to me, people that are one generation younger than I am … or a generation older"
Life stage	Life stage: One's generation is defined by the maturity of its members	"I don't think I would ever lie about my age, but I would like them (older colleagues) to perceive that I am more mature than how old I am."
Age-based	Common categories: Generations are understood primarily by the four biological age groupings (Y, X, Baby Boomers, and Veterans)	"Generation Y … they don't want to work … They don't want to move out from mom and dad. They want to stay as long as they can. They feel entitled a little bit. I wouldn't say there's something overly great about the characterizations of Generation Y … You've got the Baby Boomers who have such a huge reputation and they're in the news all of the time. I don't know that there's a whole lot being said either positively or negatively about Generation X."
	20–30-year span: A new generational grouping occurs every 20–30 years	"I tend to go with the actuarial 20-year span of groupings of people."
	Younger/older: Generations are best understood as two distinct groupings: young and old	"I think the younger generation, their mothers were—they had a little bit more respect for—we weren't just pregnant and cooking dinner, not to them. So I think I get more respect and consideration from the generation behind me."

(Continued)

Table 2.1 (Continued)

Category of understanding	Details	Illustrative quotes
Identity	**Generational identity:** Salient generational categories or groupings can be labeled as "identities," which individuals can draw upon	"I almost think of (Generation X) as being a generation without a great sense of identity, just like the name Generation X."
	Identification: Individuals identify (or not) with the stereotypical traits of a particular generation	"For me, Generation Y—I feel like I'm a little too old for it. But, the part that I identify probably most with Generation Y is the idea of … independence within the workplace seems to be a theme within Generation Y. That's something that I identify with. The thing I don't identify with is the sense of entitlement."
Contribution	**Contribution:** Generations are understood as groups of individuals who make some distinguishable impact on society	"Our dedication to work and to goals. I think that stands out in our generation … as far as 'the common good of society.' Donating time, volunteering."
Ambiguous/ Irrelevant concept	**No (or limited) value:** Examining generations has limited practical value	"When you spread it (the concept of generation) to broader social issues, you have to come up with some way to do it … But I'm not sure they really hit the nail on the head."
	Intrageneration variation: There are many differences that exist between individuals within the same generation	"I see some older people who act very immature and I see younger people who act very mature. I don't think I can (define generation)—again, I don't stereotype by age or by attitude or belief or whatever you want to call it."
	Personality: Individuals' personality has greater explanatory power than a generational grouping	"I think it's all based upon the values that are inherent within the person no matter what the generation is."

Adapted from (Urick, Hollensbe, and Fairhurst 2017).

Age Cohorts

Most attention on generations, especially from a pop-culture perspective, has focused on a biological age—based approach. In this approach, individuals of certain ages, dictated by the year in which they were born, encompass a generation and are given a generational label. Perhaps this seems obvious as a definition of generation; but, as will be discussed later in this chapter and as Table 2.1 suggests, there are quite a number of ways of defining generation. Not all of these definitions exclusively draw on age, though all use age as at least a partial component of understanding the concept of generation.

As discussed in Chapter 1, popular generational groupings or categories based on birth (from youngest to oldest) currently in the workplace include the following (Smola and Sutton 2002):

- Generation Y (also commonly known as Millennials): born between early 1980s and early 2000s according to most sources; stereotyped as lazy, entitled, and tech-savvy
- Generation X: born between early 1960s and early 1980s according to most sources; stereotyped early on as slackers, now considered a "sandwich generation" who may best serve as conduits of knowledge between generations (Urick 2017); often thought to seek work–life balance
- Baby Boomers: born between early 1940s and mid-1960s according to most sources; often currently stereotyped as conservative, unchanging, and stable, though this is a marked difference from earlier stigmas, when the generation was identified as "hippies" in their earlier years
- The Veteran Generation (often occasionally called "Silents"): born before the mid-1940s according to most sources; there are comparatively few members left in the workplace.

Some researchers and popular press articles also discuss Generation Z (who are known by a variety of other names as well, since a consensus has not emerged yet on what to call this group), born after the early 2000s. Stereotypes are still swirling around as to what expectations society and workplaces might have when considering Generation Z. As this group has not entered the workplace (at least not yet in force) at the time of writing this book, I won't mention this label or grouping much here. As for other writings on generations at work, most have not yet discussed this group either, but instead focus on the first three generations noted in the bullet points above, as these are the most prevalent in modern workplaces.

Much of the research done by business academics has focused on defining samples of workers that they study based on the age groupings that have been suggested by the previous popular generational labels (Lyons and Kuron 2013; Parry and Urwin 2011). In these research pieces, researchers seem to somewhat arbitrarily select cutoff years while largely sticking to the conventional popular generational categories, as noted earlier. Though it would appear from the popular press that generational differences do exist based on these groupings, in a comprehensive analysis of generational differences regarding job satisfaction, commitment, and turnover intentions (aspects that are often assumed to be different between generations by business academics/researchers), generational researcher David Costanza and his team (Costanza, et al. 2012) found few significant differences among members born within the common generational categories, a finding that suggests that categories based on age alone may not be the most useful way to understand generations. Nevertheless, a strictly age-based conceptualization defined by birth year is common. While other definitions of generation (noted below) recognize a time-based aspect to understanding the concept of generation, this approach brings age to the forefront. In the following, I'll note other approaches to understanding generation that assume characteristics in addition to age.

Collective Consciousness, Family, and Maturity

Beyond age cohorts, generations have also been defined by collective consciousness, family, and maturity level. I group these together in this section because, though they are not the most common way of understanding generation, they've been discussed somewhat frequently (at least in sociological academic literature). They were detailed in Table 2.1.

Based on Mannheim's sociological theory (Mannheim 1970) discussed in Chapter 1, society and members of a particular generation perceive oneness with a generational "gestalt" and believe that the collective characteristics of a generation generalize to all individuals who are encompassed by the generational label. In this view, members of each generation (as a collective) encounter some event(s) early in their lives that ultimately shape their understanding of the world and distinguish them from other generational groupings (Joshi, Dencker, and Franz 2011). According to this theory, this shared experience of events occurring during formative years sets a generation's values, motivators, and characteristics, thus demarcating where the generation begins and ends (Schuman and Scott 1989). Such a demarcation may or may not fall in line with specific birth years. After all, people may respond to the same event as a formative experience, yet be of a different biological age. Examples of such events can range from shocking (9/11, the Challenger explosion) to deeply affecting over the long term (Vietnam War, Great Recession) to the mundane (gas prices, popular motion pictures).

The genealogical definition of generation represents generations as a lineage. As with the concept of lineage in a family, one's generation is determined by where she or he fits with regard to familial succession (Joshi, Dencker, and Franz 2011). The concept of lineage has potential usefulness in a business environment (even in nonfamily businesses) such as when describing the succession of a role. For example, CEO succession, in which the title, responsibilities, and perhaps some values passed from one CEO to another can represent an organizationally based nonfamilial lineage. A CEO might be described as "third generation" if they are the third CEO of an organization.

Generations have also been defined according to common or shared rites of passage. In this view, individuals at a particular life stage experience events that contribute to their maturity (Joshi, Dencker, and Franz 2011). Such events or rites of passage influence membership of a generation by including all those who experienced such events together or nearby in temporal proximity to be a part of a particular generational grouping. In the workplace, this might occur when a group of people (a generation) enter an organization and complete orientation at the same time (Joshi, Dencker, et al. 2017).

Identities

An alternative to the above definitions is to view generations through an identity framework. According to renowned researcher Aparna Joshi and her colleagues (Joshi, Dencker, and Franz 2011), from an identity perspective, generation is based on the way in which individuals define themselves (or others) by drawing on their membership in various social groupings that are significant to them.

A key feature in Joshi's and colleagues' (Joshi, Dencker, and Franz 2011) definition of generational identity is "membership," which is related to how people classify themselves (Tajfel and Turner 1985) and perceive identification, belonging, or oneness with a group (Ashforth and Mael 1989). Generations can be seen as social identities, "that part of an individual's self-concept which derives from his knowledge of his membership in a social group (or groups) together with the value and emotional significance attached to that membership" (Tajfel 1979). In forming a generational identity, individuals often leverage some of the other understandings of generation that have been previously noted.

Thus, unlike other definitions, generations as identities are not confined to particular events, roles, cohorts, or age groups—though this perspective suggests that individuals might draw on any of these in informing their generational identity. In fact, it is likely that individuals draw upon multiple aspects in defining their generation. They incorporate these aspects into their definitions of self or others. Also (as will be shown later in this chapter) individuals often discuss aspects of belonging and self-definition when describing generation as further evidence that an identity basis to understanding generation could be useful. Since such social identities are pivotal in the development of how people and groups interact both inside and outside organizations (Hogg, van Knippenberg, and Rast 2012), understanding generations as social identities allows us to understand why people make "us versus them" comparisons between perceived generational groups. Keep in mind that, just because research has shown that clear differences were not always found between the common age-based generational categories in the workplace, people are likely to continue to use stereotypes associated with these labels to inform their generational identity, because they are common in both organizational and societal discourse.

Individuals may identify closely with a particular generation as a result of seeing the membership with a certain group's related discourse/ stereotypes as being consistent with their views of who they are as a person. For example, when defining themselves, individuals could draw on an age group (such as "Baby Boomer") in which collective memories are shared (like Woodstock, for example) to form a generational identity that draws extensively from the age-based understanding of generation that was previously noted. Membership in a social group of individuals who experienced Woodstock (assuming that these individuals are of a similar age) could therefore become the basis of their definition of their generation.

Individuals can also identify with roles and, more specifically, with how roles relate to each other (Ashforth, Harrison, and Corley 2008; Sluss and Ashforth 2007). When individuals draw on relationships with those who have preceded or succeeded them in a particular role (related to the genealogy-based generation noted above) in defining themselves, this generational membership category forms the basis for their definition of generation. For example, in the realm of science fiction, Captain Picard and his team in the popular "Star Trek" series were defined as "The Next Generation," as they followed Captain Kirk and his team as the crew of the *USS Enterprise*.

Finally, when individuals draw on a set of organizational experiences and outcomes that they share with a group of new recruits in an organization (such as experiencing orientation together, which is a life stage-based generational identity) (Ashforth and Mael 1989; Brickson 2000), this membership forms their generational definition.

Such social identification stems from several things, including the categorization of individuals as members of certain groups or roles; the distinctiveness and prestige of the group or role to which an individual perceives their own membership (known as the in-group); and the recognition and salience of other different nonoverlapping groups or roles (known as the out-groups) (Ashforth and Mael 1989). Note the relevance to the dramaturgical approach that was discussed in the previous chapter. People will try to enact expected generational behavior only if that group is valued in a context; that is, it's likely that the group is perceived as an in-group to influential individuals and decision makers in an organization. If one's generational identity is perceived as an out-group to those with power in an organizational context, individuals may either begin to disidentify (more on this later) with this identity or try to act in a way that disconfirms its associated stereotypes.

With the possibility of crafting an identity in an organizational context in a manner that is perceived to be positive, could it also be the case that the more an individual understands discourse on generations so that they enact expected behaviors the more they actually begin to identify with that generational category? It's entirely possible. Identification occurs when an individual values a group or role, possibly because they see a benefit to being a part of this group, and furthermore, they might begin to perceive this group as contributing to a sense of self. Because of the attachment of value and emotion to a group or role is part of identification (Ashforth, Harrison, and Corley 2008), individuals may begin to perceive similar values between generational members and themselves, which will continue to make their identification with a given generation stronger and encourage them to continue to enact expected behaviors. If one highly identifies with the group or role, the individual will readily draw on it as an identity in defining the self (Haslam and Reicher 2006) and will act accordingly. Of course, this usually occurs only when an individual is exposed to discourse that is related to an identity, such as a generational category.

With regard to generations, while an individual might draw upon the various generational understandings noted above to define self and others, individuals often use the most socially accepted generational understanding of the age-based approach, whose generational labels would include the Baby Boomer or Generation X designations. From these categories, individuals can group themselves and others into certain generational designations. Various researchers (Ashforth, Harrison, and Corley 2008) postulate that such categorization fulfills the two basic human needs of inclusion and differentiation (Brewer and Brown 1998) and, because some generational stereotypes are so strong and well-understood, a generational label can help to fulfill these needs. Thus, people classify themselves and others into generational groups as a result of their perceived oneness with the thoughts, values, and stereotypes popularly associated with their members to benefit them in some way, including the hope of achieving both belonging and uniqueness.

Individuals can perceive a psychological bond (or identification) with a generational group in the absence of physical contact (Deaux 1996) with others in that group. An individual may closely identify with the prototypical characteristics of a particular generation, but may not have much interaction in the workplace with others who belong to that generation. As Mannheim (Mannheim 1970) notes, even though there may not be a close personal social bond between members of a generation, individuals may identify with a generation because of a shared consciousness stemming from similar experiences within a larger social group such as the workplace as a whole or society at large.

The above discussion might sound theoretical, but it has been supported by real-world practical research. I've worked extensively on research related to generational identity with colleagues from various universities throughout the United States and Canada (as well as throughout the world) to study such issues. To examine generation through an identity framework, one of my major projects entailed conducting a qualitative study with researchers from the University of Cincinnati, in which we began by asking a sample of professionals who were diverse in age, occupational role, industry experience, educational level, gender, length in the workforce, and career stages to tell us about how they defined generation. The individuals we studied were drawn from two different pools: a young professional sample participating in a leadership training program conducted by a large Midwestern United States chamber of commerce, and a group of mature professionals who volunteered at a not-for-profit small business consulting organization with a chapter based in a mid-Atlantic city. In total, we analyzed interviews from nearly 60 individuals.

Though age varied greatly among the members of our sample, the majority of our interviews were with individuals from the oldest and youngest generations that are currently in the workforce. This is beneficial to learning more about generational phenomena, because one generation is the source of most new job entrants, while the other is the source of significant cumulative organizational knowledge. Examples of some of the interview questions that were analyzed to understand how our interviewees understood generations include:

- When someone says the word "generation," what do you think of?
- What does this word mean to you?
- What are some ways to describe your generation?
- Does this fit you or not fit you?
- What do you believe are some differences between generations?
- What are some similarities?

In the interviews, I deliberately did not define the term "generation," yet the idea that generations could be identities that are readily used to define the self or others clearly emerged in the interviewee responses.

In each interview, I found many passages related to generation identity and identification with generations (among other phenomena, which we will explore further later). Some major themes emerged regarding generations as identities, including the findings that generations can be strong identities, clear evidence of identification with generational identities, and disidentification with and de-prioritizing of generational identities. I explore each of these areas below. For the sake of brevity, I'll paraphrase the quotes and stories from our discussions in the presentation below while maintaining the spirit of what was stated. For a more elaborate presentation of our study's data on generational identity beyond that included in Table 2.1, including presentations of interviewees' statements in their own words, I suggest that interested readers examine the 2014 book chapter I co-authored with Dr. Elaine Hollensbe, an expert on qualitative research from the University of Cincinnati, in *Generational Diversity at Work: New Research Perspectives* edited by Dr. Emma Parry, one of the preeminent scholars on generational phenomena in the workplace, from Cranfield University in England.

Generations as Strong Identities

There are at least two parts to the term "identity": it answers the self-referential questions "who am I?" (individual identity) and "who are we?"

(collective identity) (Ashforth, Harrison, and Corley 2008). As previously mentioned, individuals draw on group membership, such as a generational group, to develop a sense of who they are (Tajfel and Turner 1985). In order for an individual's identity to be influenced by a generation, that group must have features that resonate with an individual's beliefs and values; or, at the very least, possess features that benefit the individual in some manner by being a member. My research team and I found that individuals perceived generations as having unique identities that were quite strong (i.e., clear, easily recognizable). For example, several interviewees noted varying levels of strength when discussing age-based generational descriptors.

To illustrate, one of the study participants, a 26-year–old male, plainly noted that the Veteran and Baby Boomer labels have clearer identities than do younger generations, such as Generation X, due to being anchored to major historical events (such as Woodstock). In his elaboration, this participant drew on multiple generational understandings when describing identity strength. In his response, he leveraged both age-based categories and collective consciousness by suggesting that events (like Woodstock) help form an identity while, at the same time, describing age-based generational labels (i.e., Veterans, Baby Boomers, Generation X) through an identity lens (i.e., associating both with membership and self-definition). The larger point, however, is that from his and others' perspectives, some of the popular generational designations have clear identities.

As an example of younger generational categories not having clear identities, one older male participant noted that Generations X and Y are completely man-made labels that he has heard discussed, but that he does not accept. His statements reinforce the idea that popular categorizations of generations are a collection of labels that, though "man-made," are recognizable social groupings made familiar through understanding societal discourse. Though this particular participant does not accept these identities as useful or accurate, he recognizes them all the same. Such recognition can unconsciously set expectations for how generational members are believed to behave, despite the potential for individuals to not consciously accept the generational groupings as legitimate.

With some exceptions, such as the statement detailed in the previous paragraph, most interviewees clearly articulated various traits and characteristics that are associated with generational identities and agreed with such characterizations. For example, some common descriptors of "younger generations" including "entitled," "me-focused," and "short term-oriented" were noted by interviewees and tended to agree with many of the stereotypes of age-based groupings present in organizations and society. In particular, the perceived identities of younger generations were most often based on stereotypical traits or characteristics that members of the groups were often assumed to possess, despite there being no clear evidence of these traits (Costanza, et al. 2012; Parry and Urwin 2011). Therefore, when considering at least some generational identities, attributes that people might believe to be defining features of a generation may, in fact, be based on perceptual errors. This occurred more frequently in my interviews for members of younger generations who have often had negative stereotypes used to describe their group characteristics (by all ages of interviewees, not just the older participants).

Participants reported various characteristics of particular generations as defining salient generational groups. Identities of generations have been reinforced either through perceptions (or misperceptions) of specific traits, behaviors, or linkages to historic events. However, some generational groupings did not have as strong or recognizable identities as others, which suggests that there is some variability in the strength of generational identity.

Identification with Generations

Identification occurs when individuals attach part of their own self-definition to a larger group. They perceive themselves as having characteristics similar to the prototypical characteristics of that group (Ashforth, Harrison, and Corley 2008; Ashforth and Mael 1989). When asked to discuss their definitions of generations, some participants in my study noted that generations are groups with which individuals can identify or find a connection.

As an illustration, a 76-year–old female participant noted that generation is more than just age. To her, it included identifying with a place, significant life events, and historic societal events. While her statements include age-based and collective conscious-based aspects of generation, they include many other complex elements of generation, including physical location, as a basis for identification. This makes sense when considering whether or not similar generational categorizations exist in different geographic regions (the United States and Turkey, for example; Urick and Arslantas 2018) as generational perceptions, generational groupings, generational characteristics, and even the definition of the word "generation" are likely to differ based on physical location. Additionally, it is often assumed that generations are based on formative years or when an individual "grew up."

As another example, one of the participants from the younger sample (age 25), linked his perception that Generation Y is adept at using technology with his own self-definition. He identifies with this generation because he is also personally good with technology. In his and other participants' statements, he regularly used "we" when discussing a generational grouping as evidence of his own generational identification. Participants regularly discussed various traits or collective characteristics that they associated with particular generations, as well as the extent to which they accepted and internalized those traits and characteristics and used these to enact stereotypical behaviors. In other words, if a generational category has expected characteristics that are appealing or familiar, individuals will draw on these characteristics in defining themselves. In my interviews, I consistently noted instances in which participants clearly stated that they identified or connected with a particular generation, which were often evidenced by discussing their own generational group membership.

Based on the prevalence of using age as a basis for defining generations (Costanza, et al. 2012; Joshi, Dencker, and Franz 2011), it is perhaps logical that age would also be a basis for identifying with a particular generation. However, some of our interviewees indicated that they do not identify with their particular birth-year generation, but that they identify more with a generation other than the one into which they were born (i.e., someone being a Millennial by birth, but identifying more with the expected values and behaviors of the Veteran generation). In other words, they viewed the concept of generation as fundamentally an identity issue.

As an example of alternate (non-birth-year) generational identification, a 30-year–old female participant noted that, though she has a biological age suggesting her membership in Generation Y, she instead identifies with Generation X. Even though this individual understands herself as being part of an age-based generational grouping (Generation Y), she does not feel that she closely identifies with its assumed characteristics; rather, she identifies with another generational grouping. Thus, in some cases, knowledge of other generational groupings' perceived characteristics allows individuals to identify with generational groupings other than those that one's biological age might suggest.

As a personal example, I am technically on the cusp of Generation X and Generation Y (depending on which particular birth cut-off years are used in the publication that you read) but identify with neither of their stereotypical traits. Though I don't necessarily identify with the label Veteran (or other terms for this particular older grouping, including Silents or the Mature Generation), I am drawn to elements that I associate with that generational category. For example, I was close with my grandfather while growing up and I believe that he passed on a lot of his values to me, with which I closely identify. Furthermore, in addition to my academic career, I lead and perform with a swing band that often plays big band music from the 1940s or earlier (a style popular with individuals with birth years that correspond to the Veteran generation)—this is something that I consider unique to someone such as myself who grew up in the 80s.

In many instances, individuals tend to identify with generations with which they are both familiar and that might be of benefit to their career in some way (note again the connection to Goffman's dramaturgical approach discussed in the previous chapter). In determining the generation that an individual will identify with, it may be the case that those generations with the strongest collective identities in the minds of the individuals are likely candidates to serve as a basis for identification.

Disidentification with and De-Prioritizing of Generational Identities

The opposite of identifying with a generation is disidentifying with a generation. Disidentification is when an individual defines oneself as not having the same attributes that he or she believes define a particular group (Elsbach and Bhattacharya 2001). Several of the interviews that my research team conducted highlighted individuals criticizing, rejecting, or disavowing aspects of a generation into which they saw themselves falling (usually with regard to the generational grouping that corresponded with their biological age). In many cases, interviewees made statements along the lines of "that's what my age group is like, but it doesn't describe me." Some people may do this because, as Goffman (Goffman 1959) suggests, disavowing one's generational membership may allow an individual to benefit within a given context. As a result, a person will try to engage in behaviors to overcome particular negative generational stereotypes.

For example, one 69-year–old male participant who has been involved with technology throughout his career described his generation as shying away from computers and technology; yet, in his statements, he distanced himself from others of his age by suggesting how much he used technology, thereby disidentifying with this generational attribute. He was not alone with his statement in distancing himself from a trait that some would perceive to be a negative characteristic of a generation. In my research, I've seen many participants, especially those of younger age groups, clearly using tactics to disidentify with their generation on the basis of contradicting their own personal level of laziness, negative job performance, and lack of community involvement, as well as other particular traits often ascribed to their generational age group. In every instance, participants would state that their generation behaved in a certain manner, but that they personally did not.

In other examples, some participants even disidentified with their generation on the basis of how they interacted with other generations. For instance, a 78-year–old female interviewee criticized others in her generation for not supporting, mentoring, or respecting younger generations, which are crucial activities necessary for organizations to continue to succeed, as will be noted later in this book. Throughout our conversation, she clearly provided examples of how she personally did support and attempt to understand those in younger generations, thus disidentifying with and distancing herself from her perceptions of her own age-based generational grouping.

Generational identities can be so well recognized that individuals might acknowledge their prototypical traits, yet distance themselves from these characteristics. Again, I suggest that distancing oneself from the traits of a generation is most likely to occur when doing so will benefit the individual in some way. In some cases, rather than disidentifying outright with a generation, interviewees established a hierarchy of identities where they valued some memberships more than others.

For example, a 33-year–old male participant described how he would feel if someone criticized his generation. He noted that one's generation is just one of many ways in which a person might define him- or herself. In his response, this participant placed generation low on the list of things that are important to who he is. Thus, by establishing an identity hierarchy, individuals may disavow association with a generation's perceived features in lieu of other more valued identities. Another participant, a 28-year–old female, elaborated more on deprioritizing generation by stating that her generation is less important than other ways she would describe herself. In particular, younger interviewees repeatedly distanced themselves from Generation Y (and its other label "Millennials") in their list of groupings that they would identify with, often because of some of the stigmas associated with being young or inexperienced in the workplace.

Individuals do not solely define themselves by one group to which they belong, but instead maintain a variety of social and personal identities upon which they draw to create their concept of self. According to the research team of Glenn Kreiner, Elaine Hollensbe, and Mathew Sheep (Kreiner, Hollensbe, and Sheep 2006) who investigate identity-related issues in the workplace, personal identity boundaries can overlap with those of group identities and individuals pull from multiple groups to which they belong in order to create a holistic understanding of their identity. This, of course, causes an individual to prioritize some groups while deprioritizing others; in effect, creating an identity hierarchy. Many of the conversations in my group's research included individuals who deprioritized their generation with regard to defining self when considering multiple identities or groups in which they might be a member. However, these same interviewees often prioritized the generation of others by emphasizing stereotypical generational values or behaviors when attempting to make sense of their perceptions of workplace colleagues.

It is clear that many of the interviewees in my research included membership in particular generations in their own self-definitions. In some cases, they discussed generation as a strong identity, identified with various generations (though not necessarily those based on their own birth year), or chose to disidentify with or de-prioritize generation as part of their identity. Yet, adding an identity discussion to other potential ways of understanding generation is not the only way that complicates an in-depth understanding of generation. Below, I discuss some additional findings from the research that I conducted along with Dr. Hollensbe. In interpreting the results, leadership and communication scholar Dr. Gail Fairhurst (also from the University of Cincinnati) was instrumental in helping to make sense of our findings. The below additional ways of understanding generation were relatively new to the academic literature and, as such, were not widely discussed until our 2017 article in *The Journal of Intergenerational Relationships* (Urick, Hollensbe, and Fairhurst 2017).

Other Ways of Understanding "Generation": Contribution and Irrelevancy

Continuing with the research sample described above, an additional understanding of generation emerged in statements that were primarily made by older interviewees. This additional understanding not previously explored in academic literature was that of "contribution," meaning that a generation emerges when a grouping of people makes a particular impact that is usually positive in nature, either on society or within organizations. Perhaps older participants in our study were more likely to have been a part of making a societal contribution than younger participants who have, to date, had less of an opportunity or a shorter amount of time to create positive change. As a result, younger interviewees were not likely to define "generation" in this way.

An example might illustrate how "contribution" informs one's generational identity. Mature participants (meaning those who had been in the workplace for many years or decades) of various ages identified with the generational category Veterans, although they were not necessarily born at a time that places them in that particular age-based generational category. This was due to their contribution of serving in the armed forces, with the positive view that they kept the country safe during times of crisis. This differs from the previously addressed concept of collective consciousness, because this understanding as contribution emphasizes that a generation has actually accomplished something or added in some way to the progress of society or organizations in a positive manner. The idea of collective consciousness could be more passive, whereby generational members just witness an event or occurrence during formative years.

However, military service was not the only contribution that my conversations suggested could be used to define a generation. Several interviewees also discussed heavily influencing industries, products, and services that are now taken for granted. One example statement from a member of the older interviewees noted making a contribution to the airline industry, which influenced society by changing the speed at which people could travel. Some other specific examples include volunteering to improve communities and creating structure and procedures for their employers that have guided workplace practices in subsequent years.

Viewing generation as being based on a contribution is in line with research that suggests that groups of people become more cohesive when they accomplish something together (Dion 2000) or, perhaps, are at least knowledgeable of the contributions of people that an individual perceives to be similar to one self. However, this was not the only new understanding of generation to emerge in my research.

The second new understanding of "generation" also came primarily from the older interviewees. A large number of the mature participants in my study stated that understanding generations is of little use. In fact, to them, the idea of "generation" is as an ambiguous or irrelevant concept; the concept of generation is not important because it is meaningless. Though past researchers have pointed out that the concept of generation is unclear (Costanza, et al. 2012; Parry and Urwin 2011), much of society's discussions on generation are based on an assumption that understanding generational phenomena is both important (Lyons and Kuron 2013) and that the definition of generation is clear. In contrast, many of my research conversations called these assumptions into question, as several of the older interviewees noted the media's role in propagating age-based generational labels, though they were meaningless to some of the people I spoke with.

Similarly, several interviewees stated that "generation" is an ambiguous concept because there are many differences that exist between individuals with similar birth years. It would seem to these individuals that a certain generation marked by common birth years is not homogenous in nature. Some participants cited personality differences as an example of individual traits that suggest the uniqueness of each person within a generational age grouping.

Though individuals of various ages noted that individual differences exist, it was interesting to see that our younger interviewees were more likely to discuss stereotypical generational traits, as though generations were a strong concept with only a few individuals who did not fit into the typically accepted generational stereotypes. On the other hand, it was mostly the older interviewees who stated that individual differences were more important than generational categories or labels. Perhaps this could be related to more exposure to media sources that emphasize generational stereotypes for younger interviewees and less exposure for older interviewees. Alternately, the older interviewees may have had more experience in working with a variety of generations, so that they had examples of colleagues whose personality did not match the stereotype. Interestingly, though, the older interviewees were equally likely to leverage generational stereotypes in interactions and conflicts, even though several reported that they found generational categories to be of little use in their statements.

The fact that generation remains a "fuzzy" concept, which includes many aspects that may or may not be drawn on when considering the characteristics of individuals of different generations, makes interpreting intergenerational phenomena difficult. Still, many popular press reports (and indeed some academic researchers and empirical studies in the business realm) largely ignore the complexities of the generation concept and focus on age-based cohorts, perhaps because doing so is common to popular societal and organizational discourse. However, one of the major purposes of the book is to suggest that this overreliance is inappropriate, as it can create several negative outcomes.

Thus far, I have clouded the concept of generation quite a bit—so much so that we seem far removed from popular discourse on the topic. I will not resolve this cloudiness herein, as this is not the task of this book. However, what I will suggest is that the popular discourse on generations is not accurate. Yet, practically speaking, such discourse sets perceptions that people act on in various situations within the workplace. Therefore, it is useful to understand generation from the perspective of popular culture in order to consider others' (and our own) potential expectations of perceptions of individuals of certain ages/generations. The concept of generation becomes even more complex when considering that each individual is likely to draw on several of the above meanings in unique combinations and ways, which means that everyone's personal definition is likely to be somewhat different.

Nuanced Understandings

The people who I spoke with drew articulately upon the understandings noted above. However, there were obvious differences in the understanding of "generation" from person to person. While this lack of consensus clouds the definition, popular discourse has moved on with a simplification of the term "generation" that draws from age alone—perhaps since, as I note below, age seems to be the only common aspect of each person's understanding. Therefore, even though there are several distinct ways in which people understand generation, "generation" is still a "fuzzy" concept, because of the nuances of understanding. Similar to the concept of leadership (Kelly 2008), generations likely represents a "blurred" concept with different meanings that share a vague commonality: age (Wittgenstein 1953).

Nearly all participants drew from more than one of the meanings from Table 2.1 in describing their understanding of generations (for example, age and identity were often used in combination). One participant in the older sample summarized this well upon being asked for his definition when he explicitly said that he thinks about generation in a number of ways. Similarly, others drew from multiple perspectives, which signals the use of more than one way of understanding the broader concept.

In one example, an interviewee in the older group describes generation as an identity by suggesting that it's something that can be identified with. Additionally, she discusses generation as a collective consciousness by understanding history due to experiencing the same events during their formative years. Similarly, she also draws on lineage when she places the understanding of her generation in the context of where she falls in her family (i.e., her parents and her children).

While some participants tended to accept multiple ways of understanding "generation," others were aware of multiple meanings, but chose not to accept them (thereby further illustrating the understanding of generation as an ambiguous or irrelevant concept). Several participants reported being aware of media influences on generation (including labels and categories), but rejected them (ambiguous/irrelevant understanding) in favor of focusing on the genealogy concept of generation. Thus, even those who defined generation as ambiguous or irrelevant often relied on additional definitions, even though they rejected the overall concept of generation. As a result, each person is likely to have a unique definition of generation: a point that has been oddly overlooked in much of how generation is discussed in popular culture.

There were some additional differences in how interviewees in both samples defined generation. Specifically, older participants were more likely to view generations as a reflection of the genealogy definition, focusing on family. Additionally, while both samples relied on "age" as a basis for defining generation, they did so in very different ways.

Genealogy

As noted above, genealogy is the understanding of generation in which generation is defined as being within the context of a family—but this understanding was not understood by interviewees of all ages. In fact, this definition of generation was primarily identified by older individuals, as it was not typically mentioned by younger participants. One reason is that perhaps the genealogy concept of generation might not be salient to younger individuals because many have not started families of their own yet, which was a point stated by the younger interviewees. In contrast, many of the participants in the older sample were clear that, to them, generations were synonymous with family life. Similarly, participants in the older sample used a genealogical definition to state that they can only be familiar with their generation by knowing the generations that precede and follow them. While this is apparent within a family, it can also occur in an organization. It is likely that a jobholder has knowledge of those who were previously in the role and maybe even those who will succeed them in that position.

Age

Though both samples used age as a method to categorize generations, they did so in distinct ways. In conversations with younger interviewees, the four-generation categorization scheme (i.e., Millennial/Y, X, Baby Boomer, Veteran/Silent; Society for Human Resource Management 2005) was widely discussed.

Though younger participants did use age-based generational labels, these age-based categories were not salient to members of the older sample, who either incorrectly explained or mislabeled their membership in one of the four categories, if they heard of these categories at all (one individual whose birth year fell squarely within the Veteran category was adamant that his date of birth reflected an individual born in the Generation X age range). However, a lack of familiarity with common generational designations does not mean that the older interviewees did not draw on age to help understand "generation." Instead, they were often likely to define a new generation as occurring roughly every 20 to 30 years without articulating a clear age-based label.

Though all interviewees of all ages referenced age in different ways, there were some commonalities evident in nearly all our conversations. The most frequent commonality was labeling generations dichotomously as either "younger" or "older."

The finding that age can be relied on in a number of ways in order to understand generations is of utmost importance because, when organizations provide training on generations that references age-based categories (or when books are published leveraging these labels), some individuals may not be aware of these labels or cannot clearly understand the timespan that they indicate. These labels are often presented in such trainings and publications without them being completely clear about their definitions, though such presentations often seem to instruct others that their currently held definitions are inaccurate. Thus, this simplification brushes over the complexity inherent in each individual's intuitive understanding of generation. This is what sets common discourse: people forget their own intuitive complex understandings of generations and abandon them for less complex stereotypical presentations, since these are prevalent in training, the popular press, and society at large. By suggesting that individuals understand generation using simplified age-based categories instead of capturing a more complex approach, discourse surrounding generations is doing a great disservice to the workplace and society. The broader implications of this simplified discourse are discussed in the next chapter.

Summary

Myths are "fuzzy" with their details. They attempt to explain some phenomena, but exact dates, locations, and other specifics are often not provided in the stories. Likewise, definitions of "generation" seem to be fuzzy, at times drawing on different aspects of understanding in unique and individualized ways. As such, people are speaking different languages, like what happened in the Tower of Babel myth after the builders attempted to build a tower to heaven. Societal and organizational discourse has emerged that simplifies such complexities by considering generations solely as age groupings.

This chapter illustrates the multiple ways in which people understand generational phenomena. Specifically, I highlight:

- There is a predominance of age cohorts in defining "generation" in popular discourse.
- Other understandings of generation might be useful to understanding the complexity of generations. Such understandings include relating generations to collective consciousness (members of a group have had similar experiences and perspectives because they were exposed to common events, despite potentially possessing different biological ages), family (generations are understood in the context of lineage), and maturity (in which generational members emerge because they experience a similar major milestone or life event at the same time, despite their biological age).
- Even more emergent in research is the understanding that generations could be viewed as identities in which individuals can strongly define themselves by a generational label. Alternately, individuals can reject a particular generational

label, thereby disidentifying with or deprioritizing this aspect of their self-definition.

- Research has also shown that some individuals intuitively view the concept of generation to not be useful when explaining behaviors, values, and differences among and between people, while others state that a generation emerges when a group of people have made a major contribution to society or organizations.
- Most individuals tend to incorporate age in some manner with several other approaches to understanding generation in unique ways. Thus, each person's understanding of generation can potentially be nuanced from others' understandings.

Managers might be interested in gaining knowledge of how their workforce understands generation as they attempt to guide related discussions and potential training on generational differences. Furthermore, business professionals should use the complexities presented in this chapter to help them examine the truth in statements on generations that they see or hear in popular use. Questioning whether or not such statements fit one's own generational understanding can go a long way toward creating positive interactions and workplaces, because doing so requires individuals to move beyond a superficial understanding of generations based on stereotypes alone.

In the next chapter, I explore how both nuanced understandings and an overreliance on age stereotypes can be detrimental to multigenerational organizations.

CHAPTER 3

Misunderstandings, Biases, and Stereotypes

Myths often help to form the ways in which the people of a culture experience and understand phenomena around them. Sometimes, a myth becomes so ingrained that it persists, even though a culture knows it to be incorrect. Consider the classic myth of Paul Bunyan from the American tradition of tall tales. In versions of this myth, Paul, a gigantic lumberjack, helps to form the Grand Canyon, as well as various lakes and mountains. Obviously, today we know more about the formation of these natural phenomena and don't believe that they were formed by a huge lumberjack and his blue ox; and yet, his story persists. The image of Paul Bunyan is often used for marketing tourist attractions and lumber-related products and has appeared in popular culture depictions as varied as children's cartoons, video games, movies, and comic books. I would wager that a majority of Americans know who Paul Bunyan is, and do not consider his myth as fact, because it is ultimately inaccurate with its simplification of complicated phenomena and explanation of how the land was formed.

Like the myth of Paul Bunyan, when it comes to generations, many people also know about generational stereotypes because they simplify complicated phenomena. However, in the case of generations, the myths are sometimes taken as fact. This causes many individuals to focus on simplicity, rather than on the complexity of intergenerational phenomena that was described in the previous chapter.

With all of this discussion on the complexity of the generation concept, one might ask: so what? In this chapter, I suggest that, despite being a phenomenon that is intuitively understood with complexity in the minds of individuals, the pervasiveness and overuse of generational stereotypes in defining generations in popular social discourse has caused our society to rely on "default" stereotypes of age groups, which is to its detriment.

Implications of Multiple Understandings

Chapter 2 reported that participants held multiple definitions of the term "generation," as no participant identified only one understanding, but rather multiple understandings. Such variability in terms of definitions reinforces the concept's ability to "stretch" and explain events. In essence, multiple definitions reflect a lack of clarity and detail, in much the same way that myths like Paul Bunyan's expand, change, or encompass new stories over time.

The details of Paul Bunyan's story change depending on the various interpretations of his myth. For example, people attribute different lakes or mountain ranges to his credit without agreeing on the specific details of their creation. Multiple versions of myths allow people to choose the version that they think has the most explanatory power for the phenomena that they see. Similarly, multiple meanings for "generation" enabled our interviewees to engage in identity work (i.e., negotiating how they define themselves and others within a particular context) and intergenerational conflict, which was intertwined with identity issues when "us versus them" generational tensions emerged because they had ready arguments, stories, and terms related to "generation" from which to draw on. Thus, they relied on the versions of the generation myth to which they were exposed, and these related statements often helped to construct their individual identities and object to or distance themselves from generational "others" who were not in their perceived in-group.

Furthermore, the statement that understandings of "generation" are highly localized, nuanced, and "fuzzy" is important because it calls into question as to why popular discourse is often simplified to exclude genealogy, maturity, and collective consciousness to focus on age groups and popularize the Millennial/Gen X/Baby Boomer/Veterans (and perhaps emerging Generation Z) groupings.

Hopefully, an acknowledgment of such complexity will spill over from academia to the business world to inform businesspeople who are writing blogs and articles on the topic and hosting training events so that their picture of generational phenomena will be more precise. The more nuanced understanding of generation that is presented here suggests a need for each person reading a publication, attending a training event, or exposed to rhetoric surrounding generational issues at work to be sensitive to and identify the aspects of generation that are being discussed, written about, or taught. However, this sensitivity is not addressed by the currently available generation-related books and trainings.

As mentioned, my research found that there were differences in the ways that members of the younger and older samples understood generations. Generations and their differences are common topics for organizational consultants and corporate-sponsored training events. This becomes problematic, however, when organizational members disagree with or misunderstand each other's concept of generation. For example, the popular age-based definition of generation (with the categories of Y, X, Baby Boomers, and Veterans) were salient to the younger sample members, but not to older interviewees. However, these categories are often used in development initiatives and jargon related to generations in general. When designing programs to train employees on intergenerational phenomena, managers will want to ensure that the definitions used are relevant for all participants, since the concept of "generation" has been interpreted in many different ways.

Though drawing on a common word (i.e., "generation"), this difference in understanding could cause both meanings and purpose to vary between younger and older employees. As a hypothetical example, consider an older employee attending his organization's training on generations. The presenter uses terms like Millennial, X, and Baby Boomer without providing clear definitions for each of these terms. In contrast, the employee has always conceptualized generation in terms of "family," and was unclear why this topic was even necessary in the workplace at all. Following the training, the employee leaves more confused than he was prior to the event. In fact, he becomes more resentful, because he has been talked to using language from which he feels excluded, particularly when other participants might be aware of the terms. This resentfulness could lead to frustration, conflict, and other negative workplace outcomes. Alternately, this participant may come to believe that his preconceived ideas on "generation" were incorrect, and instead adopts the simplified age-based category approach to understanding generation.

Reliance on Popular Culture Creates Biases

Similar to the notion of discourse, in which the understanding of a phenomena is heavily influenced by how it is talked about within a broad social background (Foucault 1977), situational contexts help set generational stereotypes and expectations that individuals have for their own and other generations. These stereotypes, in turn, influence their interactions. When individuals who might have a prior understanding of generation are exposed to an oversimplified model, they might adopt the simpler, organizationally approved definition of generation. Yet, how one interacts with other generations and understands them is not just influenced by training in her or his organization. There are other ways in which individuals are exposed to a popular culture interpretation of generation, which could cause them to change their definition and lead to biases.

For example, it is unsurprising that "media" affects how individuals understand generation, as well as how they work with others from different generations, because it helps set generational stereotypes and expectations for how members of generations should act. Therefore, in setting generational expectations and stereotypes, the media influences the nature of these interactions. In the following sections, I will further elaborate on how and why this occurs, in addition to examining other influences that impact intergenerational interactions. Table 3.1 presents a few example statements from my research that further illustrate some influences on intergenerational interactions.

Table 3.1 *Example statements of influences on intergenerational interactions*

Categories	Influences	Quotes illustrating influences
Societal context	**Economic factors:** Macro and personal economic factors such as debt level, standard of living, and buying power, among others, set the tone for the types of interactions that occur between generations often by setting values or perspectives of generational members.	"I think this young generation—when I see the younger people, they'll never live the standard of living I had because of the way the economy is."

	Media: The media portrays generations in a way that sets expectations for how generations will interact with one another.	"I think the labeling of generation is media-driven so that it gives the media a shorthand to report on various and sundry societal kinds of trends and also news stories and things like that. I think the media is the one who came up with the labels that are used, or at least they popularized the labels that are being used."
	General political/societal events and climate: Shifts in political values, macro-societal power, usage of laws and regulations, and uncertainty mark the nature of interactions by influencing perspectives of generational members.	"The difference, I think, today is that (an earlier decade) was a much simpler time. It was a much simpler time and the expectations were very clear. You knew where you stood. I think that what we've conveyed to the generations that are just starting today is unfortunately—I use the term chaos or uncertainty … Today, nothing is certain … The international situation is just terribly confused. Growing up, we knew who the enemies were of our country. Today, it is not known. So I would say what, unfortunately, we have passed down to the younger generation is a degree of uncertainty or a degree of chaos which they're learning to deal with."
Work context	**Workplace characteristics:** Organization size, structure, culture, and industry category influence the nature and types of interactions that generational members have (including either experiencing or not experiencing generational stereotypes).	"Generation Y—I don't feel personally associated with it, but I do feel like sometimes I get a bad rub: arrogant and helicopter parents, expected entitlement in the workplace. These are some kinds of assumptions that are made, and I sometimes find it frustrating. There can be strokes of truth to things, but I just think that that's just so wide an assumption. Now maybe it's because of the sector I work in."
	Work experience: Perceptions of how much work experience an individual possesses influences how they are treated in the workforce: for example, younger generations might be undervalued because they have limited work experience.	"So, if someone (goes into) Certified Financial Planning at 45 and I started when I was 22, I'll have 8 years of experience and be considered a young professional—where he's 40. People are like, 'Well, he's smarter.' You know, maybe because he's 40 he wouldn't be considered a young professional … Young is usually not a good adjective to describe something.

(Continued)

Table 3.1 (Continued)

Categories	Influences	Quotes illustrating influences
		"You know? I mean, when's the last time you said, 'Oh, it's great. They're young.'? Or … you know? A guy strikes out in baseball, it's, 'Oh, he's young, he doesn't have enough experience.' And so, when you look at young professionals, I think it's like 'Oh, he doesn't have enough experience, but he's trying.'"
Individual characteristics	**Personality and traits:** Individual traits such as personality help guide intergenerational inter-actions; some individuals leverage individual traits to influence their inter-actions.	"I don't like stereotypes because I think everybody's an individual. You can have somebody—you look at them and you think oh, God, this person will never succeed—and they do great! To me, it's what you have inside. A lot of people in my generation—'Oh, they've got tattoos, they've got piercings, they've got their hair dyed. They're no good. They're worthless. Their work ethic isn't as good,' all that kind of stuff. To me, if more people of my generation were less judgmental, there would be less of a gap between generations."
	Maturity level: The maturity level of an individual of a certain generation can minimize the importance of gen-erational stereotypes in interactions, though some may choose to focus on generational stereotypes.	"It's a maturity thing and I think that, unfortunately, sometimes our generation is looked at like we're lazy or we don't know what we're doing."
	Family upbringing: How an individual is raised (including transmitting values) or the number of generations present within a family influences the way that individuals interact with others from a different generation, often	"My generation, I—of course, I always say—we were more authori-tarian and strict. Your parents, 'This is what you're doing. This is where you're going to school. This is what you do. You go to church. These are the things you do. If you vary from them, you can get yourself in trou-ble.' And now, I've seen families on disability collecting. The father's

	by providing them with a particular perspective.	on disability. The mother claims disability. They fall into workers' comp. And the next generation up is doing the same thing. You'll see one or two or three generations collecting some type of government reimbursement. Different generations are how they perceive their parents and how their parents perceive their parents and where their values came from.'"

Adapted from Urick (2013).

Societal Context

In the interviews, participants discussed their influences, both on how they define "generation" and how they interact with members of particular generations. Some common themes included the current economic climate, media, and general political/societal events.

Both samples reported the economy as being influential to how they approach other generations. As an example, one of the interviewees from the younger sample discussed his interactions with a woman from an older generation. He believes that her upbringing in a time of a financial crisis influences her message to younger generations. From his perspective, she communicates with members of younger generations in a manner that does not resonate with them, as she drew upon her previous experiences of growing up during difficult economic conditions.

The economic situation that individuals experience early in their life characterizes their expectations of intergenerational interactions. If economic conditions are different during other generations' formative years, these interactions might lead to statements that are not appropriate, such as openly criticizing younger employees for going into too much debt when significant school loans and housing costs are often unavoidable expenses for many younger professionals.

Just as many interviewees in both samples had their intergenerational interactions influenced by the economy, interviewees also reported being directly influenced by rhetoric in popular media and news outlets. As noted by discursive analysts, such "big picture" discourses that form within a society can be drawn on by individuals as a resource for formulating and articulating ideas that are expressed in interpersonal conversations (Alvesson and Karreman 2000). Interviewees drew upon "big picture" discourses evident in the media in constructing their personal generational understanding.

The way that generations are discussed in popular culture served as a resource to interviewees in forming their own understanding of generations and how interactions should be happening—this is why public and popular discourse on generations is so important in the workplace. Many individuals draw on media descriptions and portrayals of other generations to set expectations for what members of that particular generation are like, and this heavily influences the way they interact with one another.

As one member of the younger sample noted, he feels stereotyped because older colleagues view "crap" (his term) on television, portraying his generation negatively, even if these portrayals are fictional. This particular interviewee believed that older generations have a stigma against younger generations in interactions as a result of how young individuals are portrayed on television. This was a recurring theme in the interviews: expectations influenced by the media often led to a lack of respect from older individuals with whom younger employees worked (and vice versa). Some expectations were even influenced by the media that a particular generation consumed, including the music and movies that were believed to be popular among particular age groups.

Interviewees also described political and societal events as having an impact on their intergenerational interactions. In the interviews, I noted instances of societal pressures related to the changes in government-imposed laws and regulations, an increase in uncertainty in the world, and changes in societal values. Aparna Joshi and colleagues (Joshi, Dencker, and Franz 2011) note the challenges that the transmission of values create and their relationship to difficulties and frustration in intergenerational interactions. Several of the older interviewees discussed attempting to pass down their values to younger generations, but having difficulty with doing so, as a result of societal influences.

For example, one particular older interviewee discussed his values, which were informed by his generation, and the difficulty he had in getting younger generations to buy into them. As a result of this difficulty, his interactions were impaired with younger generations who chose not to accept these values because of other societal pressures. The values noted by interviewees that they perceived to be difficult to transfer include hard work, the importance of conversation, traditional religious and conservative political ideals, and perseverance, among others. In the interviews, some societal pressures that changed over time and caused tensions included work–life balance: older interviewees stated that younger colleagues were less involved in volunteering in the community while simultaneously engaging in too many extracurricular activities outside of work. On the other hand, younger interviewees suggested changing societal expectations related to what was expected of them while lamenting a lack of work–life balance.

Societal influences are one resource that interviewees drew on to set the stage for how members of generations interacted with one another. Broad factors such as economic situations, the media, and more general political and societal shifts all influence intergenerational interactions. Individuals draw on these larger contexts as resources to enact their intergenerational interactions. For example, older interviewees preferred those values that were important in the society in which they grew up, and rejected values they perceived to be "newer," even if the newer ideals seemed to become more important or accepted as society shifted. Younger interviewees accepted and embraced newer values, while perhaps overlooking the values of older generations.

Work Context

In addition to a broad societal context, work context issues were cited as being influential in people's interactions with other generations. These influences included workplace characteristics and culture, as well as past experiences in dealing with other age groups at work.

Interviewees often mentioned the culture of an organization as either facilitating or hampering intergenerational interactions. Culture can be thought of as those underlying assumptions, values, and artifacts that strongly influence the behavior of organizational members. Interviewees also referenced the size of the organization in influencing levels of respect between members from different generations. For example, smaller work groups were reported to facilitate interactions efficiently and effectively across multiple generations, which, in turn, helped organizations to achieve optimal results. Such constructive interactions among generational members were not as evident to the interviewees when considering larger groups. Perhaps not having enough group members from one's own generation in a small group to get work done made positive intergenerational interactions crucial; in other words, people had to rely on individuals of all ages to ensure that group goals and objectives were met. Also, given the small numbers of individuals of a particular generation within a smaller group, forming in-groups and out-groups would probably be less likely. Finally, smaller groups would ensure more frequent contact among generations, because intergenerational interactions would often need to occur in order to get work done.

Other interviewees cited industry characteristics as influential in their intergenerational interactions. Intergenerational interactions may be more challenging when older people try to break into an industry that is dominated by younger employees, such as in a technologically advanced industry, perhaps because individuals believe that they might need to work harder to create positive interactions in their environments, for example. Industry characteristics are important to consider because some employees may never experience negative intergenerational interactions, due solely to the characteristics of the industry in which they work. However, other industries may be characterized by more challenging or negative interactions, which may depend on the typical age of the workforce.

As an example, a younger interviewee explained that he was essentially forced to network with members of an older generation in order to get ahead due to the nature of his industry. He reported challenges with this requirement and noted that he had to make connections and find commonalities in any way that he could. Just being there and making face time (this concept will be explored more in the section on resolving interaction challenges) could go a long way toward earning respect from his point of view. As a result, the type of industry, "an aging workforce" full of "old white guys" (in his own words), influences his interactions, as he feels the need to "find commonalities" to fit in.

Additionally, interviewees of a variety of ages reported that past work experiences either added to or detracted from the quality of interactions with other generations. Part of this is likely because people draw upon previous experiences when setting their expectations of others at work. Generally, having more experience with other age groups in the workforce was seen as facilitating more interactions characterized by respect and positive outcomes. One older interviewee notes that members of younger generations respect him for his years of experience and this, in turn, leads to interactions in which learning occurs. He viewed his long experience in his organization as a reason why younger individuals look up to him, because they don't have as much experience. This was a common theme among several interviewees.

On the other hand, having worked in a particular context also gives employees a certain perspective. For example, individuals might develop a bias about the type of employee needed to fulfill job roles (for example, perhaps they must be of a certain age). This perspective can often negatively inform interactions with other generations. Thus, work context influences the nature of intergenerational interactions. From the interviews, it was clear that culture, size, and industry of the workgroup were important work context factors that have an effect on how workplace intergenerational interactions take place.

Individual Characteristics

I also found that interviewees referred to individual characteristics in describing their intergenerational interactions. Specific individual-level factors that emerged include one's personality, maturity level, and family upbringing. Some interviewees relied on individual characteristics in their interactions with other generations particularly in cases in which they minimized the importance of age-based generational groupings and generational stereotypes. One reason for this finding may be that, as "disbelievers" in age-based prototypical traits or behaviors (such as those associated with the common generational categories), they had fewer expectations of what members of other generations should be like. They may have also been less likely to consciously enact stereotypical traits or behaviors of their own generation—perhaps even consciously trying to be wary of confirming generational stereotypes.

Several interviewees reported not letting generational stereotypes guide their interactions with individuals. In many instances, parties of intergenerational interactions noted that one's individual characteristics were more influential in interacting with other generations. In one example, a self-described member of the Baby Boomer generation disregards the generational labels of others, especially if he feels he can learn skills like technological proficiency from "younger people." This person clearly showed the personality dimension of openness, a trait associated with willingness to engage in new experiences (McCrae 1996), which is more often attributed to Millennials and Gen X-ers. Several older interviewees noted differences within their generation on this dimension, in that some Baby Boomers are open to learning technology while others are not. As a result, even a single individual personality characteristic (such as openness to learning) can affect the ease with which someone is likely to engage in interactions with other generations.

Another characteristic that is unique to individuals is their maturity level. One's personal level of maturity was often perceived as being important in influencing an interaction. As evident in one example, when asked about his experiences in working with other generations, one interviewee notes that maturity levels vary between individuals in generations by suggesting counterintuitively that some older individuals act immature, while younger individuals act mature. As a result of this, individual differences in maturity (rather than generational categories) are more important to this person because they explain individuals' willingness to interact with each other. Individuals who are perceived to be immature would also be perceived not to be team players, and these resulting interactions, if clouded by such perceptions, may be stressful or difficult.

Additionally, both younger and older interviewees remarked that their intergenerational interactions were influenced by their upbringing and were often related to their formative years with their family. In some instances, interactions were influenced by the generations in which they were brought up by or alongside. According to interviewees, younger individuals who were close to individuals in more mature generations during their formative years were often more likely to adopt (or at least understand) an older individual's values in the workplace. Younger individuals who understood or accepted values that were important to older individuals were less likely to experience negative interactions with older individuals in work interactions.

Similarly, as will be elaborated on later, spending time with others in a different generation tends to create positive perceptions of that generation and can lead to positive interactions. As an example, one of the younger interviewees noted that her parents were from an older generation and, as a result, she was able to effectively interact with members of that generation. Having grown up with parents older than those of her peers, this younger interviewee drew on her family experience. She identified more with "morals similar to older people" since these were morals she internalized as a child and drew on as an adult. These values inform her workplace interactions with other generations.

In the above examples (and throughout the interviewees' comments), I noted relationships to multiple understandings of generation. Three of the understandings of generation apparent from this discussion are irrelevancy, maturity, and genealogy/family, which influenced the interactions with other generations in the examples provided. In the first example, the interviewee suggests that maturity is different from one's biological age, which suggests that generation is not as useful a guide for interactions as is each person's own maturity level. In the second example, the interviewee noted that her views of generations were different as a result of her relationship with her "older" parents. To summarize, individual characteristics influenced the intergenerational interactions of members of both older and younger employees.

Biases Lead to Stereotypes and Prototypical Expectations

In a 2014 ThomasNet Survey, respondents pointed to a troubling shift in the workplace set to occur over the next decade (ThomasNet 2014). As older workers who possess vital expertise and different perspectives leave the workplace in force and younger employees (Millennials or the even younger Generation Z) emerge as decision makers in their organizations, they are often not adequately prepared to face crucial leadership challenges.

Part of the reason why younger workers may be ill prepared for this shift is that communication can be stifled between individuals of different ages which, in turn, minimizes the opportunities for knowledge transfer.

Such ineffective communication can occur because many employees view some age groups negatively, which can lead to workplace tension and conflict. For example, experienced workers may feel that they can't effectively transfer their knowledge to younger employees, while younger employees may feel as though they aren't valued in the workplace.

These communication challenges result from biased perceptions rooted in age stereotypes, rather than clear and accurate generational differences that accurately describe each individual of a certain age. After all, the stereotypes associated with generational labels are often inaccurate. There are a lot of variations of values evident in members of the same age group, despite the popular perception that members of particular age groups all share similar values. Unfortunately, it's often such inaccurate perceptions that allow age stereotypes to influence how people interact with each other at work.

Summary

Just as there are many slightly different myths about the legendary Paul Bunyan, there are many competing definitions of generation, and these are often as lacking in truth as the tales of the legendary lumberjack. Indeed, the most common understanding of generation relies on stereotypes that continue to exist, despite that these stereotypes are not supported by research.

In the next chapter, I elaborate on why an overreliance on stereotypes and prototypical expectations is a detriment to workplace interactions. In sum, this chapter has stated:

- Having multiple understandings of "generation" causes confusion about which term is being addressed. Though each person's perspective is somewhat nuanced and wholly unique, most understandings draw on some concept of biological age. However, age groupings have been relied on almost exclusively in popular media and discourse, and this exclusive reliance blurs the complexity that individuals inherently recognize by oversimplifying conversations related to generational differences.

- Relying too much on popular discourse in our conversations on generations leads to continuing biases and stereotypes of age groups.
- Biases, then, create expectations that can lead to unpleasant interactions in the workplace.

It's likely that most (if not all) of us work in a multigenerational workplace. To be truly effective at work, it's imperative to cut through the noise of the pervasive stereotypical understanding of generational groupings. Before using generational stereotypes to influence how we approach others of a different generation, it might be useful to reflect on our own expectations and biases of other age groups in order to keep them in check. Failure to do so will lead to challenging interactions.

The next chapter will focus on how and why stereotypes, biases, and expectations lead to challenging interactions, and the implications that these interactions have in the workplace.

CHAPTER 4

Implications for the Workplace and Beyond

Many myths concern conflict, ranging from the Trojan War of Greek mythology to Ragnarök of the Norse tradition. Although workplace conflicts are usually less extreme, they are also apparent when examining intergenerational phenomena. In fact, every person with whom I spoke during the course of my research vividly described accounts of times they conflicted with members of another generation, often because one of the parties was interacting with the other under the guidance of incorrect or even offensive stereotypes.

Even those interviewees who did not label their conflict as intergenerational clearly experienced such tension. In one instance, a memorable and immediate intergenerational conflict emerged for me in a research interview. I was running just three minutes late to a meeting with one of my interviewees in the older age group, as I had run over time in my previous interview that day. When I arrived, he berated me for at least 10 minutes about the importance of being on time, especially to a meeting with someone as important as him. Despite my sincere apologies and statement that we would not waste any additional time if we could just get on with the interview, he went on to tell me that his undergraduate university's president always told his class about the importance of timeliness and that he only agreed to be interviewed because he respected my dean. He was almost turning red and I could tell by the look on his face that he was very angry.

I realized at this point that he thought I was a student! I assume that this may have been because I communicated with this gentleman via a university e-mail address. This was several years ago so I admit that I looked young at the time (but not *that* young), though I did explain in my e-mail to him that I was a *professor* doing research. When I kindly told him I was a professor, he was in disbelief. He still would not do the interview with me until I reminded him that his statements would be confidential—at which point he reluctantly signed the required research consent form and we began a civil discussion. His tone had changed. About 15 minutes into our conversation, I asked him to describe a time when he experienced intergenerational conflict and, to my shock, his statement was that he couldn't think of any times that happened. I wanted to remind him of the conversation that we had had just 15 minutes before, but I did not. I think what caused his reaction was a stereotype he may have held that younger individuals lacked professionalism and experience. Because I looked to be young for a professor, to him there was no way I could have had the experience to be a professional researcher, and instead was surely a cocky undergraduate student.

In the previous chapter, I explored stereotypes, biases, and expectations that have resulted from misunderstanding the complexity of the concept of "generation," which stems from defining generations differently and from not focusing on the inherent differences of individuals within perceived generational groups. In this chapter, I discuss some of the negative implications of this heavy reliance on stereotypes, biases, and expectations, including challenging interactions and conflict, a breakdown in knowledge sharing, and the formation of negative cultures.

Challenging Interactions

Chapter 3 explored how perceived generational differences emerge, which can create tensions or conflict in the workplace. Much of what will be discussed in the first part of this chapter is related to a study on the same groups of professionals noted earlier that I published with Drs. Elaine Hollensbe and Suzanne Masterson from the University of Cincinnati, and Dr. Sean Lyons, a renowned scholar on intergenerational workplace phenomena from the University of Guelph, titled "Understanding and Managing Intergenerational Conflict: An Examination of Influences and Strategies" in the *Work, Aging, and Retirement* journal in 2017 (Urick, Hollensbe, and Masterson, et al. 2017). In this study, there was a prevalence of workplace intergenerational conflict and tensions reported by interviewees.

First, let me define what I mean when I talk about conflict. Conflict involves interactions marked by disagreement or struggles between parties, the possibility of interference in resource allocation or objectives by an opposing party, and perceptions of incompatibility between parties (Thomas 1992). In many instances, conflicts are marked by negative interactions. Similarly, tensions are clashes that produce discomfort between parties that need to be managed (Stohl and Cheney 2001). Tension can be considered a type of latent conflict that is characterized by uneasiness, rather than outright aggression. In interviewees' responses, it was often difficult to distinguish between latent, underlying "tension" and aggressive, more overt "conflict," though all of the interviewees did describe some form of intergenerational interaction challenges. As a result, I will use these terms somewhat interchangeably. In the following discussion, I present several types of tensions and conflicts that the interviewees described. In my study, I found that conflicts or tensions were primarily based on beliefs about intergenerational values, behaviors, and identities that were influenced by biases and stereotypes of usually age-based generational labels and perceptions. In the following discussion, it is not my goal to further perpetuate stereotypes. Rather, I share the views of the interviewees that my research team examined to report perspectives (guided by stereotypes) on why intergenerational conflict occurs. Table 4.1 provides some example quotes from the interviewees as evidence of representative statements to consider in my discussion.

Table 4.1 Examples of intergenerational conflict or tension

Conflict category	Perceived generational difference leading to tension	Illustrative quote
Values-based	**Status quo vs. innovation:** Maintaining the status quo/complying with organizational policy and thinking versus resisting old ways of doing business and attempting to innovate.	"I've worked for a boss who was probably 30 years older than me and she didn't want to hear the new ideas that we had. She wanted to do everything the old way and even when new ideas were brought to her, she would go back to old ways. Even if it seems like she saw the new ideas could be better, she didn't want anything to do with them. And I had done the same sort of work for a younger

(Continued)

Table 4.1 (Continued)

Conflict category	Perceived generational difference leading to tension	Illustrative quote
		boss, and just those opinions were much more valued and things were much more efficient. The younger boss was more open to hearing our ideas."
	Traditional vs. progressive: Valuing historically accepted ideals versus being more open-minded about political values, religious beliefs, diversity, patriotism, formality, appearance, and manner of presentation (includes being reserved versus outgoing).	"I think that young professionals as a generation are more open when it comes to race and sexual orientation. I don't think anybody of a younger generation really sees an artificial distinction, where some people of the older generation do."
Behavior-based	**Earned vs. entitled:** Perceiving one's own generation as having worked for the benefits that they possess, while perceiving another generation as expecting to be given things without truly earning them (includes issues related to purchasing on credit, wanting outcomes immediately, and levels of proactivity).	"The people that I started to see come into the workforce, instead of looking for an opportunity to succeed, it was: 'What can you offer me? What am I getting out of this job?' rather than 'What can I contribute to this and make a success out of?' … It was 'What kind of benefits do I get? When do I get my first raise? How many weeks of vacation do I get?' It was all 'What do I get from working for you?'"
	High tech vs. low tech: Leveraging technology in the workforce versus more traditional means of doing work (also includes tensions related to ability to use technology and lack of recognition for technology development)	"The young people today! It's a whole different world of technology and I just don't feel part of it."

	Skilled vs. unskilled communication: Perceiving one's own generation as having strong communication skills while perceiving another generation as being unable to communicate effectively (includes issues related to willingness to listen as well as challenges communicating in networking situations).	"We use phones for phone calls to talk to people. The next generations are texting and Facebooking and things like that and I think that's a big difference. I see that as a breakdown in the communication skills …"
Identity-based	**Me vs. we:** Focusing on self as an individual versus taking a team- or others-based social approach to work (identifying strongly with a larger group or considering others' opinions).	"It's become a very much, I think a 'me' issue with that group [younger generation]. They're more 'me' oriented than they are 'we' oriented, if you understand what I'm saying … It's kind of like everyone's in their cubicle and they're all doing their thing with the data that they're working with and they're moving it on to somebody else. It's like that until the day ends. Then they go home and try to relate with their families and their friends. I'm not sure how that works … it seems to me to be a very foreign kind of existence."
	Single vs. multiple identities: defining self by multiple roles (e.g., family, volunteer work, mentoring, etc.) versus defining self by one role (work).	"… It was a couple of vice presidents talking about a potential deal and the account that they were working on from an accounts standpoint. That meeting started on Friday and it gets going into Friday afternoon—and you know they wanted to have something done by the end of the meeting or at least agreed upon. Of course things changed, so they needed the analysis to be re-run and all that. I remember one of the vice presidents saying, 'Oh, (interviewee's name) can do that. He can do that on Saturday. He's got no wife or kids or family to go home to,' sort of tongue-in-cheek. I knew where he was coming from, but to others that might have been perceived a little bit like, 'Wow—just because he's younger and doesn't have a family situation, he should not be the one working that time period.' Whatever."

Adapted from Urick, Hollensbe, and Masterson, et al. (2017).

Values-Based Tension

Values-based tension arises from the perception that each generation cares about different things (Cennamo and Gardner 2008; Smola and Sutton 2002; Twenge, et al. 2010). Based on an analysis of the interview data, two types of values-based tension emerged from interviews: willingness or resistance to change in the workplace and the adherence to or defiance of more traditional general social values.

Such perceived generational differences partially refer to maintaining the status quo or resisting (rather than embracing) change. In the samples, younger interviewees believed that they "think outside the box" or "push the envelope," but viewed older generations as wanting to maintain the current state and not challenge the way that things have historically been done. In many instances, older interviewees agreed with this statement. Some reported that members of their generation value complying with formal procedures and view members of younger generations as not tolerating structure and wanting to immediately change things unnecessarily.

In a particularly illuminating example, one young professional labeled an older generation as "complacent," and by implication, suggested their intent to maintain the status quo at all costs. In contrast, the same interviewee described himself as a "person that likes to challenge the status quo," which caused him to come into conflict with older colleagues whom he saw as rejecting this value. This dissonance creates conflict (the interviewee noted "going head to head") as intergenerational perceptions emerge and become salient in the workplace. In contrast, older interviewees describe this tension as reluctance by members of younger generations to accept things as they are, and also by their unwillingness to listen to and learn from others older than themselves. In other words, these interviewees often criticized younger colleagues for not being compliant with the rules, procedures, values, and other aspects of a company's culture. As a result, both younger and older interviewees saw valuing change as a difference between generations; but each sample framed this difference in a way that reflected positively on their own age-based generational grouping.

The perceived values difference of progressivism and traditionalism played out in a variety of ways. As a whole, older interviewees perceived members of younger generations to be politically liberal, have limited spirituality, and be less patriotic than older generations, all of which they related to progressivism. Conversely, members of younger generations perceived older colleagues to be conservative (both politically and spiritually), as well as less accepting of diversity.

One older interviewee expressed frustration with members of younger generations at work because he perceives that they do not possess the same traditional religious values that he does due to his perception that a majority of members of younger generations do not actively participate in organized religion. Additional statements from interviewees showed that this was not an uncommon sentiment. People stereotyped other generations about whether they possess traditional or progressive values related to politics, religion, and even appearance (for example, how conservatively or informally they were dressed).

Behavior-Based Tension

Behavior-based tension arises when one person attributes another person's workplace actions and conduct to their membership in a particular generational grouping. When the other person's generationally ascribed behavior conflicts with one's own behaviors or expectations, tension can emerge. There are three specific perceived generational differences that relate to the behavior-based category: earned versus entitled, high-tech versus low-tech, and skilled versus unskilled communication.

The earned versus entitled perceived generational difference was frequently reported by many interviewees of multiple ages. Members of the older sample perceived that younger generations often behaved in ways that suggested they expected things to be handed to them without hard work or effort (i.e., exhibiting entitled behavior), while their own generation has earned what they've received in life through working hard. Anecdotally, this perspective seems like a common one that has existed between older and younger generations throughout time, despite differences in specific context or generational category labels. On the other hand, younger interviewees perceived older generations as being overinvested in work and their own generation as seeking better work–life balance. As an example of the former, some older interviewees perceived younger generations as overextending their credit, a behavior that is tied to their belief that members of younger generations feel entitled to purchase certain items, despite not having the cash to buy them. Many of the older interviewees also perceived younger generations to have a short-term orientation (evident in some statements by interviewees in the older sample similar to "they want it now"), including a willingness to switch employers to get ahead, a phenomenon that was noted by interviewees of multiple ages. In contrast, older generations were perceived by both younger and older interviewees as having more stability and a lower likelihood of changing jobs.

Many younger interviewees expressed a more positive take on the entitled stereotype by noting that younger generations seek balance as opposed to overinvesting in work. A few of the young professionals I studied reported caring for small young families, which lessened the importance of work in their lives. Others reported focusing on outside activities (such as hobbies, the community, or socializing), which made their work activities less important than they are for members of older generations who younger interviewees often perceived to be more vested in work. As a result, what older generations saw as "earned," younger generations tended to see as "overinvestment" with work.

Perceptions of different lifestyles between generations create tension when younger generations become frustrated by being labeled as "not working hard enough" when, in fact, they view themselves as working smarter, not harder. In other words, younger interviewees perceived that they are also "earning" their outcomes, though perhaps they use a different manner of working than members of older generations.

Some of this difference is evident in perceptions of generations centered on leveraging technology to complete work (such as relying on software or hardware), which comprises another type of behavior-based generational tension. As one younger interviewee noted, technology is "the one big gap" between generations, and indeed, this generational difference was reported by nearly every participant in the samples, regardless of age or generation. Younger interviewees noted frustration with decreased communication and efficiency because they perceived older individuals as reluctant to embrace or leverage various technologies, such as texting, to communicate. However, this tension goes deeper than just communication-related technology issues. Some older interviewees, for example, noted that members of younger generations seem to undervalue traditional ways of doing work, because they take technology for granted.

One older interviewee, an IT manager, perceived technology use among younger generations as "just what they do." But even though he works in a technology-related field, he reported not liking technology and seemed to view it as merely a tool, which he suggests is a different perspective from his younger colleagues. Because of generational differences in technology-related behaviors, challenges arise when multigenerational teams must work together. Coordination of work may be difficult because of the reluctance or frustration that individuals experience when they feel restricted about their preferred ways to get work done through (or without) technology.

The final specific perceived behavior-based generational difference that leads to the tension noted in the interviews centers on differing perceptions by both generations about the extent to which they and members of other generations communicate in a skilled way. Older interviewees perceived a lack of communication skills in members of younger generations. They often reported frustration with younger generations' inability to communicate, which included technology-related communication issues, though these were not the only issues reported. Older interviewees suggested that problematic communication skills in members of younger generations included an inability to transmit or interpret messages effectively and a lack of tact in interactions. In many instances, this "unskilled" communication resulted in workplace challenges such as inefficiencies, conflict, unclear messages, and a lack of transmission of information. Some of the older interviewees attributed these challenges to how younger generations learned to communicate. One manager noted that he was unable to communicate with anyone in their twenties, due to his perception of their inability. This would be highly problematic, especially if this individual had a younger employee assigned to report to him.

"Skilled" communication meant something altogether different to some members of the younger sample. They viewed communication differences as arising from the older generation's failure to adapt to contemporary media. In this case, tension is illustrated through a breakdown in communication that causes frustration and major challenges in interactions, so much so that the message of communication is lost or misunderstood. Potential communication barriers between generations can result from this tension.

Identity-Based Tension

Identity-based tension arises as a result of the way that people define themselves and others or, in some cases, how they perceive the way others (perhaps those of a different generation) define them. These tensions result from competing self-definitions that people must manage simultaneously (Ashforth and Johnston 2001; Kreiner, Hollensbe, and Sheep 2006; Serpe 1987). In the interviews, participants reported tension that arose from perceived generational differences in the ways that they saw their own generation's identity and that of other generations. Specifically, these emerged as "me versus we," as well as tensions of single versus multiple identities.

I refer to the first specific identity-based generational difference as "me versus we." This tension refers to differences in how members of generations perceived that they (and other generations) gave priority to a personal identity or a collective identity. There seems to be a difference between what are termed idiocentric and allocentric personalities (Triandis, et al. 1985). Idiocentrics emphasize one's own personal goals, views, needs, pleasures, and beliefs over those of others, while allocentrics emphasize shared beliefs, perceive themselves as being similar to others, and pay attention to others as well (Triandis, et al. 1985). In other words, this tension can emerge when individuals perceive someone of a particular generation to be a team player or to be selfish.

Interviewees in both samples made me–we judgments about both members of other generations and members of their own generations. In one example, a younger interviewee pointed out a distinction between generations is the extent to which "me" or "we" is prioritized by describing the "new" (i.e., a younger) generation more idiocentrically, as being "all about me" and the "old" generation more allocentrically, as focusing on shared success. Members of both groups labeled their own generation as "me" or "we" and other generations as "me" or "we." As a result, while one generation was not consistently labeled as being "me"-or "we"-focused, all generations had both members and different generations label them both ways, although these labels were applied to describe multiple generations interchangeably.

Related to this finding, interviewees commented about how caring their own generation's members are of others, how likely they were to associate and help people within the context of a larger group, how not self-centered they were, and how likely they were to engage in mentorship. Differences in the "me–we" distinction were often discussed in conjunction with conflict and tension that arose from a lack of collaboration and teamwork.

This finding is related to three levels of identity orientations: (1) personal, defining self as a unique individual; (2) interpersonal, defining the in terms of an interpersonal relationship; and (3) collective, defining self as a member of a social group. It is often assumed that individuals have a predisposition toward a particular identity orientation, and each identity orientation has a different set of social motivations that are associated with it (Brewer and Gardner 1996; Brickson 2000). As noted by interviewees, perceptions of the particular orientation that was stereotypical of members of a particular generation caused increased conflict in the workplace, despite some evidence (Weber and Urick 2017) that indicates a large variation of predispositions within generational categories.

The second identity-based generational difference (single versus multiple identities) involves drawing on one or on many salient identities. Younger generations perceived older generations as defining themselves in one primary way (fundamentally in terms of their work role), while they identified themselves as having a variety of identities or roles. On the other hand, older interviewees defined themselves as engaging with many identities outside of work, including volunteer roles and being a member of a family; they also saw younger generations as pursuing multiple roles other than strictly their work-related one, but in these instances, these outside-of-work roles often interfered with accomplishing work tasks, to their detriment.

Differences in identity perceptions were often described in conjunction with questions asking about conflicts at work. Some interviewees expressed resentment about the way younger or older generations viewed them. This resentment went both ways: younger interviewees felt that older employees expected them to be more focused on work, while older interviewees felt that they were not seen as "holistic" individuals with responsibilities and aspects of self that existed outside of work.

Identity-based tension can arise based on how broadly or narrowly an individual defines both themselves and others. According to younger interviewees, older generations were more inclined to expect younger generations to consider their work role as the most important identity; however, interviewees in both samples tended to define themselves much more broadly than by their work role alone.

Minimization of Knowledge Transfer and Intergenerational Learning

Despite often focusing on stereotypes, the media and popular culture has also acknowledged the importance of intergenerational knowledge transfer, often in the form of mentorship. In *The Last Jedi* (Johnson 2017) episode of *Star Wars*, a modern (pop-culture Hollywood) myth, a young Rey seeks out an older Luke Skywalker as a mentor to transfer knowledge related to using the mythical force. Initially, the grizzled and careworn Luke was seemingly apprehensive of Rey as he focused on the stereotype of naivety and inexperience in their initial interactions. In the more real-world example of *The Intern* (Meyers 2015), Ben and Jules engaged in mutual intergenerational mentorship where they explored issues related to managing a business and the changing nature of the workplace. Similarly, both Jules and Ben were apprehensive about working with each other because of age-based stereotypes related to willingness to learn, technology usage, and experience. In both examples, interpersonal relationships began with conflict that might have blocked the passing on of important skills and knowledge, whether age-old Jedi secrets or expertise in managing a successful business.

Intergenerational biases, stereotypes, and misperceptions ultimately impact knowledge management, knowledge transfer, and intergenerational learning if they persist unchecked. I explore this in the article "Three Generational Issues in Organizational Learning: Knowledge Management, Perspectives on Training and 'Low-stakes' Development" published in *The Learning Organization* with Dr. Therese Sprinkle from

Quinnipiac University in 2018 (Sprinkle and Urick 2018). I draw extensively on this piece in the following discussion.

Knowledge management is the transference of specific task-related skills, as well as tacit and experiential knowledge that includes appropriate organizational behaviors and decision-making abilities, such as a consideration of culture, organizational politics, and acceptable leadership styles. The transfer of tacit knowledge, those things that are ingrained in one's mind and not easily translatable into traditional classroom-based educational events, is important to organizational survival as older generations detach from leadership positions and younger generations assume these roles. It is impossible to transfer knowledge without having effective interactions. Thus, the conflicts and tensions that were discussed earlier in this chapter negatively impact the intergenerational transfer of knowledge.

Perhaps because of these ineffective interactions, businesses report that they are unprepared for this intergenerational shift in knowledge. To illustrate, in a survey of manufacturers (ThomasNet 2014), while 63 percent of participant organizations expect growth, they also reported a lack of preparation within the organization to manage this growth properly. Part of this is due to a lack of proper intergenerational development. Of the 490 respondents, 80 percent identified themselves as between the ages of 45–65+, with nearly half expressing a desire to retire within the next decade. Despite this clear demographic shift that will occur in organizations, 65 percent of participant organizations had no clear succession plan in place to develop the next generation for leadership roles (ThomasNet 2014).

These trends are occurring in a variety of economic sectors (Stanford GSB Staff 2010), not just manufacturing. However, anticipated economic growth coupled with losing a lot of experience and organizational knowledge does not appear to be complemented by an intergenerationally focused knowledge management strategy, which will leave younger employees ill-prepared to move into leadership roles. In other words, once they are challenged to assume these roles, younger generations may find themselves underprepared for these challenges due to a lack of plans to train them properly as older employees filter out.

Organizational newcomers, often younger generations, benefit organizations because they bring in new innovative knowledge and ideas, but they are also likely to face difficulties in their ability to influence other organizational members to embrace these new ideas (Urick, Hollensbe, and Masterson, et al. 2017). Furthermore, despite the benefit of new ideas, keeping an organization's collective memory intact is important to ensure that the knowledge that is crucial for the organization's survival remains in the organization. This protects its cultural identity, knowledge of processes, and understanding of current customer expectations. Retention of this knowledge can lead to continued performance (Moorman and Miner 1998).

To support anticipated levels of growth, organizations must hire and equip younger generations with the appropriate tools. These include passing on pieces of current collective memory as well as empowering new employees with the leverage to communicate new ideas. While explicit task-related knowledge can be taught through seminars and degree programs, tacit and experiential knowledge, a deep understanding of the organization's value system can only be taught through observation, mentoring, and trial and error.

On the other hand, experienced workers (who are often from older generations) have learned a lot throughout their careers, increasing organizational knowledge as they developed; if their knowledge is passed down to newcomers, organizations can continue to function (Cook and Brown 1999). Knowledge conversion theory (Nonaka and von Krogh 2009) suggests that knowledge is an asset that should be managed by organizations to enable their ability to successfully compete in the marketplace. Three useful types of knowledge that organizations must consider include: (1) explicit knowledge, or task-oriented understandings of one's role, organizational goals, and/or enhanced techniques/software; (2) tacit knowledge, which might include cultural and context awareness, decision-making styles, and power/politics; and (3) practical wisdom or "experiential knowledge," which emanates from a holistic understanding of the impacts of a decision to the organization and to society as a whole (Nonaka and Takeuchi 2011). An organization that does not adequately prepare newcomers for leadership roles through all three types of knowledge cannot expect these individuals to lead. Yet, as noted above, challenges in intergenerational interactions will limit the transference of these types of knowledge.

Many members of a generation will often enter organizations at the same time and will fill roles at a similar level. Such newcomers are often perceived to have limited practical experience (Urick, Hollensbe, and Masterson, et al. 2017), and it is incumbent on the organization to enhance their skills. While explicit knowledge is often taught through training and development programs aimed at increasing skills, tacit knowledge and practical wisdom are more difficult to instill through such overt tactics. These must be transferred through observation, learning by doing, and trial-and-error. All of these methods require positive intergenerational interactions in the workplace. These areas of knowledge (i.e., tacit, practical wisdom) require targeted socialization tactics (Saks and Ashforth 1997) where newcomers are presented with planned, but immersive and informal, learning experiences.

Some socialization tactics can include telling stories to accentuate accepted norms, celebrations to highlight cultural beliefs, explicit indoctrination of a value system, and emphasizing behaviors to model (Schein 1991; Levitt and March 1988). Despite these tried and true tactics, messages sent and received effectively may be limited as negative generational perceptions inform the way that members of various generations communicate (Urick, Hollensbe, and Fairhurst 2017). For example, older generations may withhold information because they believe that newcomers won't care about old customs or values. Culture transference through ceremonies, role shadowing, and other events may be set aside because of these perceptions. Conversely, younger generations may perceive members of the older generation as unwilling to learn (Warhurst and Black 2015), as noted above. In many organizations, strong tensions arise between generational members, which can limit the type and quality of learning and knowledge that is passed on (Urick, Hollensbe, and Masterson, et al. 2017).

Many formal programs are built to address the perception of new employees' increased technological preferences (Urick 2017), rather than addressing the training needs of all generations. Given the above discussion, it is important that organizations build development programs that address the needs of multiple generations into their culture, rather than avoid targeted socialization programs because of perceived intergenerational differences.

Generational Differences Regarding Training

Workplace training, which is related to intergenerational learning and knowledge management, has evolved from a less hands-on focus, such as on-the-job training or shadowing, to formalized educational programs, such as traditional classroom-style events, group-based seminars and workshops, or training delivered via technology. In 2014, the Association for Training and Development (ATD) conducted a study of 340 organizations to ask about their learning trends (ATD Research 2014). ATD found that training initiatives were heavily weighted toward instructor-led formal training. Many leveraged technology that enabled learning to occur at a distance or on the employee's own time. While such training can be crucial to the transfer of explicit knowledge, which can offer newcomers education in task-oriented skills, it has generally largely ignored tacit knowledge. These modules tend to omit those pieces of learning that occur primarily through hands-on experience.

Behavior modeling is useful to passing tacit knowledge on to younger generations who may be organizational newcomers. Famous psychologist Albert Bandura's (Bandura 1977) highly cited social learning theory emphasized the need for "interpersonal learning" through the use of behavior modeling as a primary means of passing on culture and values (Warhurst and Black 2015). Organizations have recently sought to improve their technology-enabled educational offerings in order to address tacit knowledge. As a result, they have turned to technology to address behavioral modeling, rather than using a face-to-face technique, such as role shadowing, which might facilitate positive intergenerational interactions on the job. Technology-enabled instruction can be leveraged for education because learners can be engaged by having fun. These include Web-based instruction, podcasts, webinars, simple Web searches to find information on a job-related issue, and computer-enabled entertainment, or "edutainment," a type of gamification where enjoyable competitions are used to provide exposure to concepts and behaviors useful for job performance in a safe environment with no broader negative work implications (Kapp 2012).

Fun initiatives such as "gamification" can be effective, as they increase engagement and immersion while assisting learners in making the connection between concepts and a work situation that they might experience

(Kapp 2012). Games can model and reinforce appropriate behaviors at work. When training younger generations for decision-making roles, edutainment is perceived as an important formal component of behavior modeling by simulating experiences that are likely to occur on the job. As it generally focuses on younger generations, edutainment builds on an assumption that newcomers learn best through technology-enabled instruction—though it is likely that all generations might benefit from this approach.

Unfortunately, despite how well-developed the simulated experiences are and how developers hope to improve on behavior modeling, only a limited amount of tacit knowledge can be taught through simulation. Despite improvements in the field, edutainment still tends to be more successful overall when used for knowledge transfer.

Most work decisions leverage experiential knowledge (Nonaka and Takeuchi 2011), which emanates from the convergence of explicit, tacit, and practical bases of knowledge. This knowledge is most effectively built through more hands-on individualized means. Various scholars (for example, Saks and Ashforth 1997) suggest that, if it is necessary for the individual to demonstrate proactive strategies and behaviors such as those that are necessary in leadership roles in which younger generations will soon be expected to engage, individual socialization tactics like customized on-the-job training or mentorship programs are crucial.

In many multigenerational workplaces, though, vital individualized knowledge management and intergenerational training is lacking. This is likely due to a biased interpretation of generational training preferences. In 2017, I published a short study in the *International Journal of Training and Development*: "Adapting Training to Meet the Preferred Learning Styles of Different Generations" (Urick 2017). I analyzed potential trends related to organizational learning and generations, again leveraging a sample of members of both younger and older generations. I noted that, although the older sample expressed a preference for on-the-job training and mentorship, both younger and older interviewees were under the impression that younger employees would be more comfortable with technology-enabled training. Each participant carried a perception of their own and of other generations' preferences for learning and knowledge management.

In contrast, not every individual within a generational group will agree with the perceptions that others have on how they learn best. There seems to be a lack of intensive knowledge management programs that consider individual and group-oriented approaches, as well as formal and informal approaches, for a multigenerational workforce. This may prove to be detrimental to the evolving workplace. Group-based training and development has its place in the transfer of explicit knowledge (Saks and Ashforth 1997), but less formal individualized initiatives allow employees to learn behaviors that are immediately applicable to their jobs. Thus, they are a means of emphasizing necessary role-related skills and competencies. For example, one age-related study of learning (Warhurst and Black 2015) found that shadowing and observing others were most helpful in transferring role behavior. Additionally, less formalized programs help organizations achieve decreased costs; this is partially due to fewer instructor or technology development fees, but also because actual work occurs in tandem with the training (Frazis and Loewenstein 2007).

The development of mentoring programs is one option for organizations to manage both tacit knowledge and practical wisdom. Mentoring programs are neither instructor-led nor classroom-based. They are offered while both employees continue to be engaged in work. Regular meetings are encouraged to allow for behavior modeling (Wilson and Elman 1990). Having a mentor exchange knowledge with a newcomer can be useful as those with a desire to learn exhibit a preference for leveraging personal sources of knowledge (Abrams, et al. 2003), as long as an appropriate mentor–mentee match can be made.

Informal mentoring, in which the mentor–mentee self-select and have a relationship that grows into fostering development over time, certainly worked in both *The Last Jedi* and *The Intern*, and these types of programs have been found to be effective in the nonfiction workplace as well. Mentored employees are likely to achieve higher compensation, job satisfaction, and transfer of tacit knowledge (Allen, et al. 2004). Such programs also offer a dual purpose to an organization: they strengthen mentees' understanding of corporate culture through the socialization that occurs during mentoring meetings, while simultaneously providing vital information for developing leadership potential (Wilson and Elman 1990). Establishment of a mentor–mentee relationship can also remedy tension in intergenerational interactions (Urick, Hollensbe, and Masterson, et al. 2017). Intergenerational mentorship forces participants to look beyond stereotypes and to seek out experiences that the mentee may need to be successful in leadership roles. The mentee may begin to accept and appreciate the insight gained from the mentor (and vice versa), effectively breaking down negative stereotypes. It makes sense that tacit and experiential knowledge would be best transferred by minimizing the impact of perceptions of intergenerational differences.

Organizations seeking to transfer culture and values should return to the model of social learning theory described by Bandura (1977), which states that organizational members learn best through interpersonal learning. This is not to suggest that technology-enabled training should be abandoned, but rather that it should be supplemented with informal/individualized initiatives, such as on-the-job education and mentorship programs.

However, mentoring programs may not be ideal for all employees, and the organization may not be designed to effectively support a mentoring program. Organizations that are plagued by intergenerational conflict and tension will not be able to have interactions that are effective enough to allow appropriate mentoring relationships to form.

Therefore, organizations may seek to provide other experiences that instill practical wisdom, offering time to practice "live" decision making across a variety of development opportunities that will appeal to a broad set of employees and generations. Some additional ways of doing this could be through low-stakes activities, like pursuing a volunteer activity, where leadership experience is gained outside the organization. This might take the form of encouraging unpaid involvement on a nonprofit board to build leadership and decision-making expertise, for example.

Focusing on Differences Creates a Caustic Culture

Creating an inclusive and welcoming culture that truly cares about all employees is crucial for both organizations and society; yet we constantly hear about marginalization, both in our country and in our organizations. Age, or generation, is certainly one basis of discrimination and marginalization. As I discuss earlier in this book, discrimination regarding generation often occurs because of the stereotypes or misperceptions that people have heard about generational categories and their members.

Nonetheless, there are many reasons to embrace diversity, including generational diversity. One reason is, of course, the importance of respecting all of humanity. In addition, for organizations, welcoming a generationally diverse source of perspectives means that there will be better decisions, higher quality products, improved services, and other improved organizational outcomes (Cox 2001). More importantly, though, by having a welcoming and inclusive workplace, people may start to perceive similarities between each other which outweigh the previously perceived differences. However, this isn't to say that all differences, such as those that may be related to generations, aren't acknowledged. On the contrary, in workplaces that welcome inclusion, differences are appreciated and respected while still recognizing that many goals and aspirations may be shared. In other words, by working with a diverse group toward common goals, a sense of shared belonging is likely to occur (Allport 1979).

It's naive to believe that all people and every organization will willingly embrace such a workplace or society—we are likely to always see negative generational stereotypes. Indeed, evidence has clearly shown that the values inherent in some cultures don't support inclusion. There are many examples of noninclusive organizations that could be considered, and many examples of workplaces that are less tolerant of certain generational groups, as evident in the conflicts and tensions noted in this chapter.

Part of the reason why some organizations do not welcome generational diversity as much as others could be due to their cultures. To paraphrase the famous cultural researcher Edgar Schein (1991), there are three levels of culture. Artifacts represent the level that is experienced with the senses. A culture is like an iceberg, and the artifacts are like the ice visible above the water. Artifacts include behaviors, such as how people treat others. Artifacts such as behaviors of employees are built upon the values of the organization, the second level of culture, which is represented by the part of the iceberg that is below the surface. Values are what the organization cares about. If inclusion is not a core value of a culture, workplace behaviors are likely to marginalize certain groups.

Many organizations forget that there is an even bigger chunk of ice supporting the values in the depths of the water. These are an organization's underlying assumptions, the third level of culture, which are beliefs that are so ingrained in an organization that they are simply assumed and rarely discussed. In order to fully embrace inclusion of all kinds (including generation), the assumptions that influence and support values and artifacts need to include respect for all humanity. Therefore, creating a culture of inclusion starts at the assumptions level. The need to care for people—of all ages and other diverse attributes—needs to be the life-blood of organizations and societies and be the number-one unquestioned belief, from which all other values and artifacts are derived, if discrimination is to be minimized.

Deliberately changing a toxic culture does not happen overnight, and only changes that impact the underlying assumptions will last in the long term. Thus, as representatives of a culture, leaders set the tone for a culture and strongly influence whether assumptions and values are positive. However, this is only part of what is needed to change a culture. People in the organization beyond those with formal leadership titles also need to reflect respect for humanity in their values and behaviors for this assumption to spread, and only then can true change occur within our organizations and beyond. The next chapter addresses creating positive change to promote generational inclusivity and, in doing so, describes the starting steps to changing caustic workplace cultures.

Summary

Conflicts have existed for centuries and have been historically documented, as well as the subject of myth. Conflict can cause a lack of positive interaction, which is detrimental to organizations when generational tensions decrease knowledge transfer between organizational members. Luke and Rey from *The Last Jedi* and Ben and Jules from *The Intern* overcame such intergenerational obstacles and the challenge of overrelying on generational stereotypes can be overcome in real workplaces too.

In this chapter, I addressed three negative organizational outcomes of overrelying on generational stereotypes:

- Focusing on generational stereotypes, rather than the individuality of a person, causes a breakdown in communication that can lead to workplace conflict.
- Conflict can decrease the effectiveness of training, education, knowledge transfer, and mentoring between generations. However, such activities are crucial as younger generations prepare to take on more decision-making leadership roles.
- A lack of information sharing and conflict can create a caustic culture, which may make some individuals feel unwelcomed in the workplace.

Hopefully, this chapter has helped readers to identify some of the causes of intergenerational tension that they may have experienced. For managers and employees, it is useful to understand why conflict emerges in organizations, and this chapter provides some examples. Furthermore, when providing training and development initiatives, organizations must consider the structure and format of education that will be most beneficial to a multigenerational workplace. Finally, a major takeaway from this chapter for business leaders is hopefully to understand the importance of culture on whether or not interactions are positive in nature. There are solutions that can be implemented to help strengthen a culture that is more generationally diverse.

This chapter focused on a negative topic as it identifies many of the problems associated with focusing on generational stereotypes. However, the next chapter is more positive in that it offers solutions to help resolve some of these major issues.

CHAPTER 5

Changing the Game

A former executive in the energy industry read an early draft of this book. After finishing it, he told me that his major takeaway was that he questioned what he knew about generations and how his own opinions on generations were influenced by the media. He also told me that he became more aware of this as he read and, as a result, decided to be more deliberate in engaging each person (regardless of generation) as an individual to improve his interactions.

To my delight, his new approach to interactions was informed by the strategies noted in this chapter. In my own intergenerational interactions, I have consistently drawn on some of the strategies presented below. Therefore, I view this chapter to be the heart of the book, as I detail strategies noted by my interviewees that may be helpful to others as they interact.

As stated, the purpose of the book is to break down the "generation myth" so that individuals can engage in more effective intergenerational interactions in the workplace. Thus far, I have pointed out challenges with such interactions and some possible reasons as to why they may not be as effective as they could be. In this chapter, I turn toward improving workplace interactions so that this book can serve its purpose: to change the game by suggesting strategies that will transform harmful conflict into positive intergenerational relationships. I make some concrete recommendations to improve intergenerational phenomena in the workplace. First, I relate some specific strategies for improving interactions that have been used regularly by participants in my research. Next, I advocate focusing on the individual and on the job itself to improve mentorship and knowledge transfer. I conclude this chapter with a discussion on why focusing on the individual is important by citing some of my research on variability within a generational group.

Strategies for Improving Interactions

For research that I engaged in and published along with Drs. Hollensbe, Masterson, and Lyons, I interviewed many people who shared strategies on how to manage conflict with individuals that they perceived to be belonging to other generations. As in Chapter 4, I paraphrase statements from the interviews that we conducted, with sample quotes illustrated in Table 5.1. To see a presentation of additional direct quotes of interviewees in our research, refer to our "Understanding and Managing Intergenerational Conflict: An Examination of Influences and Strategies" article in *Work, Aging, and Retirement* (Urick, Hollensbe, and Masterson, et al. 2017). From the interviews, three broad categories of strategies emerged: achievement-oriented, image-oriented, and ego-oriented. Interviewees in both the younger and older samples were likely to use each strategy, except where noted below (for example, only members of the older sample reported leveraging the specific ego-oriented strategy of removing self).

Table 5.1 Example strategies for improving intergenerational interactions

Strategy category	Specific strategy	Illustrative quote
Achievement-oriented	**Focusing on communication style:** Individuals consciously flex their tone of message, communication medium, or language usage.	"When I establish a new relationship with someone from an older generation, I ask them at the outset, 'How do you prefer to communicate? Can I reach you better by phone, by e-mail? What's easiest for you?' It varies. I just like to come to an understanding with that person at the very beginning of our relationship as to how it's best to communicate. That's how I manage that potential barrier."
	Performing proficiently: Individuals refer to results or achievements that are important to other generations and that they've either recently accomplished or are planning to accomplish.	"With an executive vice president in New York, I think it was my first four months working for the company and he was really challenging me on my knowledge of what I was doing. And then, 'Well, how old are you, (interviewee's name)?' And I said ... 'If I'm able to produce for you, then that's what we need to talk about.' I think that really helps get me past that barrier of him questioning my skill set."

Image-oriented	**Being visible:** Individuals make sure that their work efforts are noticed by others by being present during normal working hours (also involves maximizing contact with those in other generations).	"I taught two courses at (university's name) for a semester and I noticed a difference there. Some professors were in and out of class and there was no interaction with their students whatsoever. I ate lunch between my two classes—using brown bags, I sat in the cafeteria. Within a few weeks, the students that I had in class were visiting, sitting at my table and exchanging thoughts, ideas and so forth. And, probably, the real interesting thing is that after about three weeks one of the girls said, 'Would you be our dorm counselor?' I said, 'Well, it's a 52-mile one-way trip.' I said, 'I'm not here on campus like a full-time professor.' I had that kind of a positive experience with students."
	Managing information to control image: Individuals use (or don't provide) select pieces information or ideas to give them or their generation a positive image to others.	"There are some businesses where being older and having a little gray hair benefits you. Maybe one is investments. People look at having experience as a good thing for a lot of reasons … yeah, so in that sense, sharing my age … you know, I wouldn't be as upfront about it because it could be a deterrent or it could hurt you. Now, in other industries like technology, computers, and all that it's used as a positive. So, it just depends on what environment I was in."
Ego-oriented	**Protecting needs:** Individuals focus on ensuring that their needs are met in an interaction.	"You hate to say, watch your back (in intergenerational interactions), but the reality of it is, be careful … we're sometimes forced to, I guess, play the game, if you will, in certain situations, but that's kind of the way it is."
	Removing self: Individuals walk away from and ignore others (or lay off/terminate them in extreme cases) to avoid unproductive interactions.	"I've probably carried a grudge and that's probably part of my generation, too. Maybe we don't speak out like we should. But I've always been able to resolve conflict and if that person annoys me enough, I don't include them in whatever I'm doing. So I resolve it by ignoring them."

Adapted from Urick, Hollensbe, and Masterson, et al. (2017).

Achievement-Oriented Strategies

Achievement-oriented behaviors are related to proving one's worth in the workforce by showing others that they can be an asset to the workplace and that they are able to achieve positive results for the organization, department, or work group. Two specific strategies are included in the achievement-based category: focusing on communication style and performing proficiently.

The strategy of focusing on communication style includes interviewees consciously choosing to portray a respectful demeanor when communicating, using particular communication channels (e.g., face-to-face, phone, or e-mail), or focusing on specific language usage that they believe to be preferred or understood by other generations.

For an example related to specific language usage, an older interviewee described using language that she picked up from her younger family members when interacting with younger coworkers. In much the same way that using organizational vernacular allows an outsider to fit in with a culture (Louis 1980), using what is believed to be generational vernacular allows a member of one generation to potentially ease conflict with a member of another generation. When considering adjusting the medium through which individuals communicated with members of another generation, a few younger interviewees made a point to make a phone call (rather than texting) to communicate with older generation employees at work, because they perceived this to be preferred by older colleagues. By adjusting their communication style, these younger generation members attempted to overcome the behavior-based conflict that could arise from perceptions of lack of communication skill.

However, with this strategy, interviewees seemed to leverage stereotypes related to perspectives on how particular generations prefer to communicate without necessarily considering the preferences of the individual with whom they are actually communicating. Because of a lack of focus on the individual and a reliance on stereotypes to attempt to resolve tension, I would expect that this is not the most effective strategy, though interviewees were not asked questions about the effectiveness of their communication. To make this strategy more effective, I would recommend adjusting communication to fit an individual's preference and not their generational stereotype. I address the importance of focusing on the individual more later in this chapter.

The second achievement-oriented strategy is to perform proficiently. Interviewees reported showing or referring to results that they accomplished (or planned to accomplish) that they believed were important to colleagues in other generations. Interviewees noted that pointing to past accomplishments and showing important results increased trust between members of various generations and could lead to conflict resolution.

One interviewee from the younger sample highlighted her accomplishments by stating that she proved herself consistently at work through excellent job performance, effectively letting her work speak for itself. She ran events for her organization when she was in her early 20's and they repeatedly went smoothly. In this way, she showed that she engaged in hard work, which helped to alleviate any tension from the earned versus entitled perceived tension, noted previously.

Performing proficiently is likely to be effective because members of different generations at work often have a common goal (or at least, they should). Many interviewees stated that collaborating with members of other generations by focusing on results that both individuals cared about helped to unite efforts. This strategy is similar to a workplace superordinate goal that helps align units that have different, and in some cases, competing individual objectives (Locke, et al. 1994). However, again, this strategy would be less effective if it leverages stereotypes about what individuals believe are results that another generation cares about, rather than specifically asking colleagues of other generations what results they are most concerned with and using these as foci. Yet, this is still likely to be a positive behavior as, even if it does not help to respond to an individual's expectations, it does help contribute to an organization in a positive way. Members of other generations are likely to respond positively to this as well, because they hopefully share common organizational goals.

Image-Oriented Strategies

The second main category of strategies is related to impression management: behaviors that individuals purposefully use to attempt to create or influence a certain aura, perception, or identity about themselves to others. In other words, these are image-related things that individuals can do to try and get others to see them in a certain way.

Image-related strategies allow employees to manage others' perceptions of them and manipulate their audiences (i.e., other generations) to appear in a positive light. These strategies are related to Goffman's (1959) dramaturgical approach, which was addressed in the first chapter. Image-related strategies differ from achievement-oriented strategies, in that image-oriented strategies concentrate on creating an image without focusing on, or perhaps without actually achieving, workplace results or objectives. Two particular types of strategies in this category include being visible and managing information to control image. As with achievement-oriented strategies, both image-oriented approaches can leverage stereotypes in attempts to improve interactions. In other words, they can attempt to manage an impression in a way that confirms or disconfirms a generational stereotype. I speculate that these actions are likely to be effective, because they seek to create a positive image independent of whether their intended audience actually holds the assumed negative perceptions to which they were developed in response. Regardless, users of these strategies attempt to improve their image in some way.

Both younger and older interviewees reported the importance of being visible to other generations. However, members of the younger generations were more likely to strategically use visibility to improve intergenerational workplace interactions. These individuals discussed behaviors such as showing they were at work during typical business/shift hours, as opposed to working flex-time or leveraging technology to work from home, which could be a strategic response to behavioral-based tension arising from the high-tech versus low-tech perceived difference noted in the previous chapter.

Additionally, younger interviewees especially noted that being visible allowed for other generations to think that they were being proactive as opposed to lazy, potentially combatting behavior-based tension associated with the earned versus entitled perceived generational difference. When discussing managing appearances in the workforce, some younger interviewees mentioned that visibility included issues of "appropriateness," such as dressing professionally in order to improve perceptions, a response to the values-based tension arising from the traditional versus progressive perceived difference that was previously discussed. By portraying themselves professionally, they attempted to create an image of a hardworking and serious professional, thus lessening the likelihood of a potential conflict-generating negative perception by someone from an older generation.

Some interviewees addressed tactics related to building a reputation of being a hard worker through visibility. In such instances, being viewed by others as a hard worker helps younger employees to overcome "entitled" perceptions. Interviewees in both samples reported that being visible and spending more time with other generations made it easier for them to interact. This is similar to the "contact hypothesis" in which exposure to out-groups (i.e., other generations) serves to minimize the influence of stereotypes. By increasing contact, similarities of others who were previously perceived as dissimilar are recognized, leading to positive interactions (Pettigrew 1998). In some instances, perceptions may be changed of the individual so that they are viewed to be different from their generation. In other cases, perceptions of the entire generation may be changed.

I also noted interviewees describing ways in which they managed information to shape another generation's view of their own generation. In some instances, interviewees reported withholding information (e.g., one's actual age) to avoid negative perceptions, minimizing age (e.g., suggesting that it is not important), or maximizing age as an advantage (e.g., conforming to generational stereotypes when they were positive or could help an individual advance in their career). Specifically, younger Millennial interviewees especially noted ways that they strategically selected particular aspects of their generational stereotype that favored their image, such as pretending to be good at technology to get a promotion.

In one example, an interviewee in the younger sample maximized the advantages of his young age to a potential client, which helped to redirect a potentially tense interaction related to his age. He noted that his age was not representative of his worth and was actually a benefit to the client, because he would be around to create a relationship and work with the client for many more years than someone older might be.

This strategy could also be related to physical appearance. As an aside, this is one strategy that I have personally used in the workplace. Earlier in my career, I was often the youngest employee with my particular role or job title in the organizations in which I worked, and when I went into academia, I found this to be even more apparent. Having usually been clean-shaven for most of my life and often wearing contacts, I grew a beard and started wearing glasses to make myself appear older and thus fit in more. I felt that, in this role, people would view me to have more credibility if I looked older. An acquaintance of mine from before I had a beard or glasses one day asked me to tell him about my research. When I talked with him about the managing image strategy, his response was, "You mean like growing a crappy beard to make yourself look older?" While he explicitly called me out on my use of this strategy, I do believe that this helped improve my intergenerational interactions.

Ego-Oriented Strategies

The third and final category of strategies for managing intergenerational conflict is related to focusing on oneself rather than on others. While previously mentioned strategies are aimed at achieving results or influencing one's image to be perceived more positively, the strategies in this category are focused more narrowly on behaviors that benefit the self. Specifically, two strategies in this category are protecting needs and removing the self.

When protecting needs, interviewees noted that they interacted with other generations in a way to ensure that their own desires and wants were being met. For example, one interviewee from a younger generation reported trying to get his way with other individuals of other generations in advancing an initiative that he feels is important. He tried to do this by ensuring that the older person does "what I want them to do" or notices the initiative that he feels is important. In this case, the interviewee actively manipulated the schedule of an individual of an older generation in order to get his way, which seemed to lessen the chance of conflict.

In other interviews, participants also noted that they protected their needs by "using" others in different ways. These could include building support for ideas by using workplace politics, leveraging formal authority in interactions to push their personal agenda, or venting or complaining about intergenerational conflict to others to help manage their approach to dealing with the conflict.

The second ego-oriented strategy of removing the self was reported much more frequently by older interviewees. Using this strategy, some members of the older sample reported walking away from interactions with younger generations to end or avoid conflict. Sometimes this was done as a result of feeling not valued in the workforce, such as when one older-generation interviewee felt "blown off" by a younger coworker. Rather than engaging in potential conflict, she decided to avoid the interaction altogether. Similarly, several other interviewees noted that they resolved conflicts with other generations by simply walking away.

Understanding the Importance of Intergenerational Mentorship

The ThomasNet (2014) survey that I referred to earlier found that a troubling shift in the workplace is set to occur in the near future. Baby Boomers with crucial expertise will leave the workplace, and younger employees, such as Millennials or the even younger Generation Z that is just emerging, will quickly be placed in roles as decision makers in their organizations. Unfortunately, many of these newer workers won't be adequately prepared to face the leadership challenges that will confront them.

One reason that they will not be prepared is because there is a breakdown in intergenerational communication. The issues that I noted earlier regarding interaction challenges that lead to conflict have minimized opportunities for knowledge transfer between the groups. Ineffective communication—and workplace tension and conflict—can occur because employees may negatively view some age groups, as previously discussed. Experienced workers, for example, could feel they can't effectively transfer their knowledge to younger employees, while younger employees may feel that they aren't valued in the workplace.

In many instances in which communication challenges occurred, biased perceptions that were rooted in age stereotypes, rather than clear and accurate generational differences, were often to blame. Society tends to label people as part of age-related groups (such as Baby Boomers or Millennials). These terms are then used as shortcuts to explain why a person acts or behaves in a certain way, even though stereotypes associated with these labels often are inaccurate. In fact, there are many differences in values among members of particular age groups. Unfortunately, however, the misperceptions are all too often known and leveraged in workplaces where they influence how people interact with each other.

Even though reduced knowledge transfer occurs when intergenerational tensions and conflicts exist, organizations must develop the next generation of leaders. Organizational leaders and their employees must improve the way they perceive all generations and develop younger workers. Therefore, improved mentoring and knowledge transfer needs to occur. In order for these initiatives to happen effectively, in addition to the strategies leveraged by individuals that I interviewed to improve intergenerational interactions, some additional strategies presented below might also help.

Consider Your Own Influences

Many things shape perceptions and biases about generational differences. As previously discussed, these influences could include society, organizations, social groups, social media, casual conversations, and anecdotal books and articles—anything that could set societal discourse on the way people talk about and understand generations. To see the sheer amount of perspectives out there on generations that could set perceptions, search for "generational differences" on the Internet. The number of hits (about 1,100,000 at the time of writing) will show how much this topic is being discussed. Readers of such websites should consider how such sites could influence the perspectives of those who read them.

The Internet presents one potential source of (mis)information, and yet there are many others. When you see or hear something about generations, ask yourself these questions to determine whether the information you receive is accurate or not:

- Is the information objective, or does it draw primarily on an emotional reaction?
- Is this just one person's perspective, or are these statements universally applicable?
- What bias might the source have?

Additionally, ask yourself whether these sources have caused you to have your own bias or to form or perpetuate inaccurate generational perceptions. If they have, it is important (though difficult) to acknowledge your own bias, question whether any previous experiences with others could disconfirm the bias and consider whether holding onto this bias will help your interactions in a positive way. Taking these recommendations to heart will allow people to move beyond stereotypes and focus on the individual.

Focus on the Individual

Organizational members can improve communications with other age groups by recognizing the variability between members of a generational category. Each person has their own unique knowledge, skills, abilities, strengths, weaknesses, and values. Getting to know members of another generation and treating them as individuals rather than focusing on an associated generational stereotype will go a long way in improving challenging intergenerational interactions. Some things that might be useful to learn about a person to improve intergenerational interactions could include the following:

- What inspires that person?
- How does that person prefer to communicate?
- What are that person's aspirations?

It's About the Job, Not the Generation

Whether an employee is an emerging or experienced professional, there's an inherent obligation in working for an organization to get a job done and meet organizational goals. Rather than apply biases to which generation should be assigned particular tasks based on perceived stereotypes and judge acceptable work behaviors for how they should be completed, employees need to work together. Draw from the expertise and experiences of all age groups to help achieve mutual goals. If employees don't focus on contributing toward mutual goals, conflicts can intensify, which draws attention away from taking care of the challenges that help a workplace succeed.

Therefore, it is equally important to develop and encourage younger employees to be successful in their roles. For younger employees, it's the

responsibility of newcomers to accept such development and encouragement. Providing and accepting development and encouragement helps
to achieve accomplishments, which could, in turn, dispel misperceptions
(such as the stereotype that members of younger generations are lazy) if
they are held by colleagues of other generations.

For these suggestions to be effective, all generations in the workforce
need to effectively communicate with one another. If the effort is one-
sided, not only will there be ineffective interactions, but mentorship and
knowledge transfer won't improve. However, if all parties from various
generations filter out misinformation and get to know each other as individuals, there will be more mutual mentoring between all ages of employees—and organizations will go a long way toward developing the next
generation of leaders.

Rethinking the Importance of "Generation"

A recent study, "Examining the Millennials' Ethical Profile: Assessing
Demographic Variations in Their Personal Value Orientations" published
in *Business and Society Review* (Weber and Urick 2017), that I worked on
with Dr. James Weber, an ethics guru from Duquesne University, suggests
some interesting findings on the consistency of traits of individuals who
are perceived to be within one generational grouping. Most prior research
on generations often groups individuals within a category by assuming
that all generational members possess the same traits, behaviors, and values (Kupperschmidt 2000). This perspective of prior research, of course,
ignores any important differences among members within the same
generational grouping. However, in our study, we found overwhelming
support that there is variation within the Millennial generational grouping related to their long-term goals (i.e., terminal values) and methods
they hope to employ to achieve them (i.e., instrumental values). Specifically, within the Millennial grouping, variations seemed to be related to:

- **Gender.** For example, women in our sample placed greater
  importance on moral and social values than the men in our
  sample. This fact is not surprising because it is consistent with

earlier research (Cagle and Baucus 2006; Clinebell 2013; Cohen, Pant, and Sharp 2001; Jargon 2014; Keyton and Rhodes 1997; Oumlil and Balloun 2008; Ross, Jr. and Robertson 2003; and Searcey 2014 among others).

- **Work experience.** The expectation based on prior research (Eweje and Brunton 2009; Valentine and Rittenburg 2007; Weber 2015) is that, with greater work experience and exposure to work environments, Millennials' values would begin to change. Our study supports this expectation. Millennials with more work experience had a significantly higher concern about acting ethically than Millennials with less work experience.

- **Role/occupation.** Millennials in our sample specializing in accounting, a profession often assumed to have a strong ethical character in the business ethics academic literature (Jeffrey, Weatherholt, and Lo 1996; Lord and DeZoort 2001; Sweeney and Costello 2011), had a competence focus (i.e., a concern primarily for being proficient at role-related tasks) rather than a moral/ethical focus. In our sample, it is also interesting to note that Millennials specializing in finance demonstrated the highest level of moral values when compared with any of the other business discipline groups that we investigated.

- **Intelligence.** While intelligence is difficult to measure, in our study we used undergraduate grade-point average as an estimate and found that Millennials in college or recently graduated with a higher grade-point average (3.30 or higher) are statistically different than Millennials with a lower grade point average (3.20 or lower) when considering their values. This finding confirms earlier research investigating the role that grade-point average may have on ethical decision making and behavior (Abdolmohammadi and Baker 2007; Gupta, Walker, III, and Swanson 2011). Specifically, we found that Millennials with a higher grade point average were marginally more likely to emphasize moral or ethical values over competency values.

With the above statements, I must be careful to not stereotype certain genders, experience levels, roles/occupations, and intelligence in the same way that I advocate against stereotyping particular generations. Yet, when taken together, these findings suggest that there are other "identities" than generation that are more important, salient, or appropriate when considering differences between people. However, a lot of popular discourse does not fully consider multiple identities. These resources tend to shortchange the complexity of individuals, glossing over them to emphasize one broad label, such as generation.

These results also highlight the importance of examining differences within, rather than just between, popularized generational groupings. They suggest that popular discourse must shift focus from age-based generational understandings to incorporating more robust conceptualizations, such as those that incorporate identities and maturity, among others (see Mannheim 1970; Joshi, Dencker, and Franz 2011; and the discussion in Chapters 1 and 2). Most importantly, our findings suggest that managers should not assume that their employees, consumers, or investors value certain things just because of their age. Rather, their treatment of employees, enticement of consumers, or appeal to investors should consider the personal values, beliefs, and preferences held by each individual person in line with my recommendation above.

The contributions of our study described above lie in both the extended exploration of the Millennial generation and their values and the in-depth investigation of variations within this generation. These insights are a critical step toward better understanding the emerging populations of employees, consumers, and investors (Agan 2013; Mims 2015; Stout 2015). Furthermore, and most importantly, my research with Dr. Weber highlights the importance of expressing restraint in generalizing characteristics across an entire generation, especially one that is grouped by birth years. For example, Baby Boomers were hardly a solitary generation, given the emergence of leaders from that population as diverse as former U.S. Secretary of State Condoleezza Rice and business owners Ben Cohen and Jerry Greenfield, founders of Ben & Jerry's. Thus, I suggest the importance of more holistically considering each individual that one encounters in the workplace. Just as there is a lot of variation within the Millennial generation, as reported by Weber and Urick (Weber and Urick 2017), there is likely to be considerable variation within each of the other popular generational labels. Therefore, relying extensively on their associated stereotypical attributes is likely to be inappropriate.

While Millennials and even younger generations (perhaps such as members of Generation Z) will continue to be powerful and emerging forces in our society, we need to dig much deeper into their cognitive processes to reveal potential variations within generational groups, beginning with their personal values. From these examinations, a clearer and yet more diverse picture of the Millennials may emerge and better aid organizations seeking to comprehend the potential pool of employees, consumers, and investors. We must also begin to do this with all generations in the workforce, as well as those younger generations who will be entering into the workforce soon.

Summary

I hope that this book helps to improve intergenerational relationships and interactions, and that is why I view this chapter to be of the utmost importance because it begins with some specific strategies related to improving workplace interactions.

To conclude this chapter, the following might help improve challenging interactions:

- There are several strategies that people have engaged in to try to remedy challenging interactions. These include focusing on achievements/results, adjusting image, or prioritizing self.
- Mentorship and knowledge transfer are likely to be improved if colleagues consider their own biases, treat each other as individuals (rather than as generational stereotypes), and focus solely on getting the job done.
- There is some emerging support to suggest a lot of variability within generational categories, which makes relying on stereotypes and biases less than optimal.

For business practitioners, I hope that the strategies presented in this chapter are useful. I encourage us all to try some of them in our

interactions—especially those strategies that we may find uncomfortable—to see if they will work in our individual unique contexts.

All of the above recommendations point to one thing: treat others,
regardless of generation, as individuals, and try not to focus as much on
associated generational stereotypes. The next and final part of this book
suggests that the recommendations made here on generation and age
might be applicable to consider when examining other areas of diversity
as well.

Conclusion

The Hope for a Better World

Myths attempt to teach something about the world. Parables often try to do the same. Parables take a story to make listeners or readers think about how its teachings could inform their own behaviors. The Christian parable of the Good Samaritan, for example, tells the story of how an individual helps a traveler who was robbed, beaten, and seemingly left to die on the side of the road. The helper did this despite being considered an outsider, as part of a marginalized group who might not likely have gotten along with the victim had they met under normal circumstances, after several other individuals of a higher status passed by the victim.

We can relate this parable to our discussion in this book in two ways. First, the helper and the victim are usually interpreted to be of different statuses; the helper is lower and the victim is higher. These statuses could have formed because of perceptions of and stereotypes relating to each person's membership in particular identity groups that might have either been viewed positively or negatively at that time. Just as I recommend leaving behind stereotypes of generational groups in intergenerational interactions, this parable seems to suggest the same.

Second, different generations may have different statuses in organizations, but we all must help each other. Therefore, this parable also relates to our discussion because we can take its major theme of helping others in need and apply it to our own lives. In this way, I suggest applying the strategies noted in this book and emphasizing the individual in a variety of situations. While this book intends to improve intergenerational interactions, some of the ideas discussed here might go a long way to improving other types of conflict that are not generational in nature.

While this book is focused on generational diversity, this final section considers whether the concepts noted throughout might be applied more broadly to other areas of diversity. In doing so, I advocate for treating each person as an individual, rather than as a stereotype of a particular identity group, whether generationally based or otherwise.

Implications for Understanding Diversity

Most of my research (and this book as a whole) focuses on generational stereotypes and intergenerational interactions. However, many other diversity studies examine ethnic, racial, gender, religious, economic, orientation, political, socioeconomic, and national identity categories in their studies on differences. Could the ideas presented in the preceding chapters also inform research that examines these identity characteristics?

Specifically, could using the strategies noted in the previous chapter help to improve communications between individuals of different racial or religious backgrounds, for example? Furthermore, can some of this book's recommendations help to improve mentorship and knowledge transfer between individuals who are diverse in other ways beside age, such as gender? Finally, though the focus of this book has largely been on workplace phenomena, do the challenges and strategies noted here have implications for how people interact outside of work and in society at large?

Focus on the Uniqueness and Humanity of Each Individual

Much of my research has focused on the impact of labeling and the perceptions that labels influence (see Chapter 2 and Urick 2014; Urick and Hollensbe 2014 for how individuals negotiate their identities based on their perceptions of generational labels common in the United States). Much of the below regarding the action of labeling is paraphrased from some blog posts that I made in 2016 and 2017 on the website of Saint Vincent College, where I teach and research, and I include them here because I believe them to be relevant and useful to this book's purpose. You can check out all of my blog posts at *The Saint Vincent College Faculty Blog* (Urick 2018).

The action of labeling refers to naming, titling, or phrasing someone to focus on only a narrow aspect of self, so that the uniqueness of the individual is lost and the inherent complexity of the group to which the label is assigned is forgotten. For example, "Millennial," "Samaritan," a role like occupation, a belief system like religion, an affiliation like political party, or a demographic characteristic like gender are all labels. Labeling individuals has had many negative outcomes in organizations (see Urick and Crandall 2012 for an example of labels setting identities, which, in turn, caused an initially disruptive conflict in a healthcare setting) and negative outcomes also occur at the societal level. For example, Rothman (Rothman 1997) writes about "identity conflict" in which people fail to see the uniqueness of each individual and instead focus on prototypical traits (that are often inaccurate) of certain social groups when interacting with others, and states that this occurs within organizations, families, teams, and societies. Such conflict occurs in organizations—indeed the focus of this book has been on how generational identities create conflict at work—but it, perhaps obviously, also occurs between regions, countries, and members of our own communities that we perceive to belong to an identity out-group.

Humans tend to like order and predictability (even if we sometimes don't admit it), and labels provide the illusion of knowing who another person is when we enter into interactions with them. The problem arises, though, when we remain focused on the label and fail to see the individual. Labels take out the uniqueness and intricacy of the individual that they attempt to describe. Discursive theory (see Baxter 2010; Jørgensen and Phillips 2002; and Potter and Wetherell 1987 for excellent discussions on discourse analysis and language usage) would suggest that the words that we use not only set expectations for traits and behaviors, but also influence interactions and relationships. This occurs so much, in fact, that organizations may use such labels to impact their employment-related decisions, voters may be influenced by labels to elect a candidate despite not truly agreeing with their platform, and news stories may focus on labels rather than individuals.

I am not the first to suggest that, rather than focus on labels that seek to isolate and divide, it would be better if we focused on labels that could unite under a common goal and more inclusive identity (see Allport 1979 for a classic discussion and Rothman 1997 for more recent examples). I've had the pleasure of playing with my band, Neon Swing X-perience, at the Hard Rock Café in Pittsburgh several times, including this past year as part of our 20th-anniversary CD release party. I saw a T-shirt in the gift store there that said "All is One." It seems like the kind of T-shirt message that you might hear at a music venue like the Hard Rock, but I like that slogan, because it suggests that each person is not just a label:

we can find the things that unify us. In other words, rather than focus on differences, seeing potential similarities in each other will go a long way to uniting us. Of course, that's not to say that there aren't differences inherent between each person, but it does allow us to focus on a more cohesive identity while recognizing (and respecting) individuals' uniqueness and perspectives.

Social identity theory, self-categorization theory, and identity conflict studies suggest that labels can lead to divisions. This can lead to stereotypes, stereotype threat, negative bias, and discrimination. Labels also influence people to not see each other as they truly are in their complexity and totality: fellow humans.

When people rely only on labels of all types (including generation) in their interactions rather than seeing a holistic picture of an individual, we will experience a negative impact. I encourage us all to try to see people more for their complexity and less for their associated stereotypes, whether they are generational or otherwise. If I think of all of the identities, roles, or labels that I use to define myself, like father, husband, son, late Millennial/Gen X'er cusper, author, teacher, consultant, researcher, musician, fencer, by my faith/religion, as a Lord of the Rings and Star Wars fan, an Italian and Polish American, and others, I see a lot of complexity in the totality of my individual that many people aren't likely to see when they first meet me. You are likely the same in being a complex individual who transcends one identity label, generational or otherwise. So is everyone else. It is vital that we seek to understand each other as complex individuals in our interactions. While doing so, perhaps some of the strategies and recommendations made here to improve intergenerational interactions and break down the "generation myth" can also help us to improve interactions between other areas of diversity and different identity groups.

Summary

Parables provide examples for particular behaviors that are meant to be applied to a variety of situations. Though this book has focused on generational labels and diversity, it is my hope that the ideas presented here can be extrapolated to be applied to other situations in which conflict might arise as well.

To conclude, I'd like to leave the reader with two points.

- This book is focused on generational categories and age groups; but is it possible that the concepts addressed here might also apply to other types of diversity?
- The bottom line is that treating people with the dignity and respect that should come with a general care for all humanity can go a long way to potentially improving our organizations, societies, and the world at large.

I would encourage everyone working in organizations to get to know your colleagues, supervisors, and direct reports on a personal basis to understand who they are. I'm not saying that we need to be best friends with everyone in the workplace, but we do need to treat each other with respect, dignity, and civility, despite generation or other identity groups to which the people we interact with might belong.

There will always be challenging workplace interactions, but it is my hope that the ideas in this book might have, even in some small way, helped readers to think about and improve upon their own interpersonal interactions.

References

Abdolmohammadi, M.J., and C.R. Baker. 2007. "The Relationship Between Moral Reasoning and Plagiarism in Accounting Courses: A Replication Study." *Issues in Accounting Education* 22, no. 1, pp. 45–55.

Abrams, L.C., R. Cross, E. Lesser, and D.Z. Levin. 2003. "Nurturing Interpersonal Trust in Knowledge-Sharing Networks." *Academy of Management Perspectives* 17, no. 4, pp. 64–77.

Agan, T. 2013. *Embracing the Millennials' Mindset at Work*. November 9, http://nytimes.com/2013/11/10/jobs/embracing-the-millennials-mind-set-at-work.html?_r=0 (accessed January 17, 2015)

Allen, T.D., L.T. Eby, M.L. Poteet, E. Lentz, and L. Lima. 2004. "Career Benefits Associated with Mentoring for Protégeé: A Meta-Analysis." *The Journal of Applied Psychology* 89, no. 1, pp. 127–36.

Allport, G.W. 1979. *The Nature of Prejudice: 25th Anniversary Edition*. New York, NY: Perseus Books Publishing, LLC.

Alvesson, M., and D. Karreman. 2000. "Varieties of Discourse: On the Study of Organizations through Discourse Analysis." *Human Relations* 53, no. 9, pp. 1125–49.

Ashforth, B.E., and S.A. Johnston. 2001. "Which Hat to Wear? The Relative Salience of Multiple Identities in Organizational Contexts." In *Social Identity Processes in Organizational Contexts*, ed. M.A. Hogg, 31–48. Philadelphia, PA: Taylor & Francis, Inc.

Ashforth, B.E., and M. Fred. 1989. "Social Identity Theory and the Organization." *The Academy of Management Review* 14, no. 1, pp. 20–39.

Ashforth, B.E., S.H. Harrison, and K.G. Corley. 2008. "Identification in Organizations: An Examination of Four Fundamental Questions." *Journal of Management* 34, no. 3, pp. 325–74.

ATD Research. 2014. "2014 State of the Industry." *Research Report, Alexandria: Association for Talent Development*. https://td.org/research-reports/2014-state-of-the-industry

Bandura, A. 1977. *Social Learning Theory*. New York, NY: General Learning Press.

Baxter, L.A. 2010. *Voicing Relationships: A Dialogic Perspective*. Thousand Oaks, CA: Sage Publications, Inc.

Bolino, M.C., K.M. Kacmar, W.H. Turnley, and J.B. Gilstrap. 2008. "A Multi-Level Review of Impression Management Motives and Behaviors." *Journal of Management* 34, no. 6, pp. 1080–109.

Brewer, M.B., and R. Brown. 1998. "Intergroup Relations." In *The Handbook of Social Psychology*, eds. D.T. Gilbert, S.T. Fiske, and G. Lindzey, 554–95. 4th ed. Boston, MA: McGraw-Hill.

Brewer, M.B., and W. Gardner. 1996. "Who Is This "We"? Levels of Collective Identity and Self Representations." *Journal of Personality and Social Psychology* 71, no. 1, pp. 83–93.

Brickson, S. 2000. "The Impact of Identity Orientation on Individual and Organizational Outcomes in Demographically Diverse Settings." *The Academy of Management Review* 25, no. 1, pp. 82–101.

Cagle, J.A., and M.S. Baucus. 2006. "Case Studies of Ethics Scandals: Effects on Ethical Perceptions of Finance Students." *Journal of Business Ethics* 64, no. 3, pp. 213–29.

Cennamo, L., and D. Gardner. 2008. "Generational Differences in Work Values, Outcomes, and Person-Organisation Values Fit." *Journal of Managerial Psychology* 23, no. 8, pp. 891–906.

Clinebell, J. 2013. "Socially Responsible Investing and Student Managed Investment Funds: Expanding Investment Education." *Financial Services Review* 22, no. 1, pp. 13–22.

Cohen, J.R., L.W. Pant, and D.J. Sharp. 2001. "An Examination of Differences in Ethical Decision-Making between Canadian Business Students and Accounting Professionals." *Journal of Business Ethics* 30, no. 4, pp. 319–36.

Cook, S.D., and J.S. Brown. 1999. "Bridging Epistemologies: The Generative Dance Between Organizational Knowledge and Organizational Knowing." *Organization Science* 10, no. 4, pp. 381–515.

Costanza, D.P., J.M. Badger, R.L. Fraser, J.B. Severt, and P.A. Gade. 2012. "Generational Differences in Work-Related Attitudes: A Meta-Analysis." *Journal of Business and Psychology* 27, no. 4, pp. 375–94.

Cox, T. 2001. *Creating the Multicultural Organization: A Strategy for Capturing the Power of Diversity.* San Francisco, CA: Jossey-Bass.

Deaux, K. 1996. "Social Identification." In *Social Psychology: Handbook of Basic Principles*, eds. A.W. Kruglanski and E.T. Higgins, 777–98. New York, NY: Guilford Press.

Dion, K.L. 2000. "Group Cohesion: From Field of Forces to Multidimensional Construct." *Group Dynamics Theory Research and Practice* 4, no. 1, pp. 7–26.

Edmunds, J., and B.S. Turner. 2002. *Generations, Culture And Society.* New York, NY: Open University Press.

Elsbach, K.D., and C.B. Bhattacharya. 2001. "Defining Who You Are By What You're Not: Organizational Disidentification and The National Rifle Association." *Organization Science* 12, no. 4, pp. 393–521.

Eweje, G., and M. Brunton. 2009. "Ethical Perceptions of Business Students in a New Zealand University: Do Gender, Age and Work Experience Matter?" *Business Ethics: A European Review* 19, no. 1, pp. 95–111.

Foucault, M. 1977. *Discipline & Punish: The Birth of the Prison*. New York, NY: Vintage Books.

Frazis, H., and M.A. Loewenstein. 2007. *On-the-Job Training*. Hanover, MA: Now Publishers, Inc.

"Generational Differences Chart." n.d. Generational Differences Chart. http://locavore.guide/sites/default/files/resources/files/GenerationalDifferences Chart.pdf (accessed August 29, 2018).

Goffman, E. 1959. *The Presentation of Self in Everyday Life*. New York, NY: Anchor.

Gupta, S., E.D. Walker II, and N.J. Swanson. 2011. "Ethical Behavior of Graduate Business Students: An Examination of the Effect of Age, Gender, GPA, and Work Experience." *Southern Journal of Business and Ethics* 3, pp. 137–51.

Haslam, S.A., and S.D. Reicher. 2006. "Stressing the Group: Social Identity and the Unfolding Dynamics of Responses to Stress." *The Journal of Applied Psychology* 91, no. 5, pp. 1037–52.

Hogg, M.A., D. van Knippenberg, and D.E. Rast III. 2012. "Intergroup Leadership in Organizations: Leading Across Group and Organizational Boundaries." *Academy of Management Review* 37, no. 2, pp. 232–55.

Jargon, J. 2014. *McDonald's Faces 'Millennial' Challenge*. August 24, http://wsj.com/articles/mcdonalds-faces-millennial-challenge-1408928743 (accessed June 9, 2015).

Jeffrey, C., N. Weatherholt, and S. Lo. 1996. "Ethical Development, Professional Commitment and Rule Observance Attitudes: A Study of Auditors in Taiwan." *The International Journal of Accounting* 31, no. 3, pp. 365–79.

Johnson, R. 2017. *Star Wars: The Last Jedi*. Directed by Rian Johnson. Produced by Walt Disney Pictures.

Jørgensen, M., and L.J. Phillips. 2002. *Discourse Analysis as Theory and Method*. Thousand Oaks, CA: Sage Publications, Inc.

Joshi, A., J.C. Dencker, and G. Franz. 2011. "Generations in Organizations." *Research in Organizational Behavior* 31, pp. 177–205.

Joshi, A., J.C. Dencker, G. Franz, and J. Martocchio. 2017. "Unpacking Generational Identities in Organizations." *Academy of Management Review* 35, no. 3, pp. 392–414.

Kapp, K.M. 2012. *The Gamification of Learning and Instruction: Game-based Methods and Strategies for Training and Education*. San Francisco, CA: Pfeiffer.

Kelly, S. 2008. "Leadership: A Categorical Mistake?" *Human Relations* 61, pp. 763–82.

Keyton, J., and S.C. Rhodes. 1997. "Sexual Harassment: A Matter of Individual Ethics, Legal Definitions, or Organizational Policy?" *Journal of Business Ethics* 16, no. 2, pp. 129–46.

Kooij, D., A. de Lange, P. Jansen, and J. Dikkers. 2008. "Older Workers' Motivation to Continue to Work: Five Meanings of Age: A Conceptual Review." *Journal of Managerial Psychology* 23, pp. 364–94.

Kreiner, G.E., E.C. Hollensbe, and M.L. Sheep. 2006. "On the Edge of Identity: Boundary Dynamics at the Interface of Individual and Organizational Identities." *Human Relations* 59, no. 10, pp. 1315–41.

Kreiner, G.E., E.C. Hollensbe, and M.L. Sheep. 2006. "Where Is the 'Me' Among the 'We'? Identity Work and the Search for Optimal Balance." *The Academy of Management Journal* 49, no. 5, pp. 1031–57.

Kupperschmidt, B.R. 2000. "Multigeneration Employees: Strategies for Effective Management." *The Health Care Manager* 19, no. 1, pp. 65–76.

Levitt, B., and J.G. March. 1988. "Organizational Learning." *Annual Review of Sociology* 14, no. 1, pp. 319–38.

Locke, E.A., K.G. Smith, E. Miriam, D.O. Chah, and A. Schaffer. 1994. "The Effects of Intra-Individual Goal Conflict on Performance." *Journal of Management* 20, no. 1, pp. 67–91.

Lord, A.T., and F.T. DeZoort. 2001. "The Impact of Commitment and Moral Reasoning on Auditors' Responses to Social Influence Pressure." *Accounting, Organizations and Society* 26, no. 3, pp. 215–35.

Louis, M.R. 1980. "Surprise and Sense Making: What Newcomers Experience in Entering Unfamiliar Organizational Settings." *Administrative Science Quarterly* 25, no. 2, pp. 226–51.

Lyons, S., and L. Kuron. 2013. "Generational Differences in the Workplace: A Review of the Evidence and Directions for Future Research." *Journal of Organizational Behavior* 35, no. S1, pp. S139–S157.

Mannheim, K. 1970. "The Problem of Generations." *Psychoanalytic Review* 57, no. 3, pp. 378–404.

Maurer, T.J., F.G. Barbeite, E.M. Weiss, and M. Lippstreu. 2008. "New Measures of Stereotypical Beliefs about Older Workers' Ability and Desire for Development: Exploration Among Employees Age 40 and Over." *Journal of Managerial Psychology* 23, no. 4, pp. 395–418.

McCrae, R.R. 1996. "Social Consequences of Experiential Openness." *Psychological Bulletin* 120, no. 3, pp. 323–37.

Meyers, N. 2015. *The Intern*. Directed by Nancy Meyers. Produced by Nancy Meyers.

Mims, C. 2015. "How Aging Millennials Will Affect Technology Consumption." *The Wall Street Journal*. May 17, http://wsj.com/articles/how-aging-millennials-will-affect-technology-consumption-1431907666 (accessed June 17, 2015).

Moorman, C., and A.S. Miner. 1998. "Organizational Improvisation and Organizational Memory." *The Academy of Management Review* 23, no. 4, pp. 698–723.

Nonaka, I., and G. von Krogh. 2009. "Perspective—Tacit Knowledge and Knowledge Conversion: Controversy and Advancement in Organizational Knowledge Creation Theory." *Organization Science* 20, no. 3, pp. 481–683.

Nonaka, I., and H. Takeuchi. 2011. "The Big Idea: The Wise Leader." *Harvard Business Review* 89, no. 5, pp. 58–67.

Oumlil, A.B., and J.L. Balloun. 2008. "Ethical Decision-Making Differences Between American and Moroccan Managers." *Journal of Business Ethics* 84, no. 4, pp. 457–78.

Parry, E., and P. Urwin. 2011. "Generational Differences in Work Values: A Review of Theory and Evidence." *International Journal of Management Reviews* 13, no. 1, pp. 79–96.

Pennell, J. 2018. "Barack Obama pays touching tribute to former political opponent John McCain." *Today.* August 26, https://today.com/news/obama-pays-tribute-former-political-opponent-john-mccain-t136303 (accessed August 26, 2018).

Pettigrew, T.F. 1998. "Intergroup Contact Theory." *Annual Review of Psychology* 49, pp. 65–85.

Pilcher, J. 1994. "Mannheim's Sociology of Generations: An Undervalued Legacy." *The British Journal of Sociology* 45, no. 3, pp. 481–95.

Potter, J., and M. Wetherell. 1987. *Discourse and Social Psychology: Beyond Attitudes and Behaviour.* Beverly Hills, CA: Sage Publications.

QuotesGram. n.d. *Quotes About Generational Differences,* https://quotesgram.com/quotes-about-generational-differences/ (accessed August 29, 2018).

Ross, W.T. Jr., and D.C. Robertson. 2003. "A Typology of Situational Factors: Impact on Salesperson Decision-Making about Ethical Issues." *Journal of Business Ethics* 46 , no. 3, pp. 213–34.

Rothman, J. 1997. *Resolving Identity-Based Conflict In Nations, Organizations, and Communities.* San Francisco, CA: Jossey-Bass.

Saks, A.M., and B.E. Ashforth. 1997. "Organizational Socialization: Making Sense of the Past and Present as a Prologue for the Future." *Journal of Vocational Behavior* 51, no. 2, pp. 234–79.

Schein, E.H. 1991. *Organizational Culture and Leadership.* San Francisco, CA: Jossey-Bass.

Schuman, H., and J. Scott. 1989. "Generations and Collective Memories." *American Sociological Review* 54, no. 3, pp. 358–81.

Searcey, D. 2014. "Marketers Are Sizing Up the Millennials." *The New York Times.* August 21, http://nytimes.com/2014/08/22/business/marketers-are-sizing-up-the-millennials-as-the-new-consumer-model.html (accessed February 21, 2015).

Serpe, R.T. 1987. "Stability and Change in Self: A Structural Symbolic Interactionist Explanation." *Social Psychology Quarterly* 50, no. 1, pp. 44–55.

Sluss, D.M., and B.E. Ashforth. 2007. "Relational Identity and Identification: Defining Ourselves through Work Relationships." *The Academy of Management Review* 32, no. 1, pp. 9–32.

Smola, K.W., and C.D. Sutton. 2002. "Generational Differences: Revisiting Generational Work Values for the New Millennium." *Journal of Organizational Behavior* 23, no. 4, pp. 363–82.

Society for Human Resource Management. 2005. *SHRM Generational Differences Survey Report: A Study by the Society for Human Resource Management (SHRM Surveys Series)*. Survey, Alexandria: Society for Human Resource Management, VA.

Sprinkle, T.A., and M.J. Urick. 2018. "Three Generational Issues in Organizational Learning: Knowledge Management, Perspectives on Training and 'Low-Stakes' Development." *Learning Organization* 25, no. 2, pp. 102–12.

Stanford GSB Staff. 2010. "Research: CEO Succession Planning Lags Badly." *Insights by Stanford Business.* June 1, https://gsb.stanford.edu/insights/research-ceo-succession-planning-lags-badly (accessed February 24, 2017).

Stohl, C., and G. Cheney. 2001. "Participatory Processes-Paradoxical Practices:-Communication and the Dilemmas of Organizational Democracy." *Management Communication Quarterly* 14, no. 3, pp. 349–407.

Stout, H. 2015. "Oh, to Be Young, Millennial, and So Wanted by Marketers." *The New York Times.* June 20, http://nytimes.com/2015/06/21/business/media/marketers-fixation-on-the-millennial-generation.html (accessed March 15, 2016).

Sweeney, B., and F. Costello. 2011. "Moral Intensity and Ethical Decision-making: An Empirical Examination of Undergraduate Accounting and Business Students." *Accounting Education* 18, no. 1, pp. 75–97.

Tajfel, H. 1979. "Social Categorization, Social Identity and Social Comparison." In *Differentiation Between Social Groups: Studies in the Social Psychology of Intergroup Relations (European Monographs in Social Psychology)*, eds. H. Tajfel, 61–76. London: Academic Press.

Tajfel, H., and J.C. Turner. 1985. "The Social Identity Theory of Intergroup Behavior." In *Psychology of Intergroup Relations*, eds. S. Worchel, and W.G. Austin, 7–24. Chicago, IL: Nelson-Hall.

Thomas, K.W. 1992. "Conflict and Conflict Management: Reflections and Update." *Journal of Organizational Behavior* 13, no. 3, pp. 265–74.

ThomasNet. 2014. "ThomasNet's Industry Market Barometer." *ThomasNet.* November, http://thomasnet.com/pressroom/Industry_Market_Barometer.html (accessed February 24, 2017).

Tolkien, J.R.R., C. Tolkien, and H. Carpenter. 2000. *The Letters of JRR Tolkien.* New York, NY: Mariner Books.

Triandis, H.C., K. Leung, M.J. Villareal, and F.I. Clack. 1985. "Allocentric Versus Idiocentric Tendencies: Convergent and Discriminant Validation." *Journal of Research in Personality* 19, no. 4, pp. 395–415.

Twenge, J.M., S.M. Campbell, B.J. Hoffman, and C.E. Lance. 2010. "Generational Differences in Work Values: Leisure and Extrinsic Values Increasing, Social and Intrinsic Values Decreasing." *Journal of Management* 36, no. 5, pp. 1117–42.

Urick, M.J. 2017. "Adapting Training to Meet the Preferred Learning Styles of Different Generations." *International Journal of Training and Development* 21, no. 1, pp. 53–59.

Urick, M.J. 2013. *Intergenerational Interactions in Organizations: A Grounded Theory Examination*. Doctoral Dissertation, University of Cincinnati, Cincinnati: University of Cincinnati.

Urick, M.J. 2018. *Saint Vincent College Faculty Blog*. http://info.stvincent.edu/faculty-blog/author/michael-urick (accessed November 25, 2018).

Urick, M.J. 2017. "The Aging of the Sandwich Generation." *Generations* 41, no. 3, pp. 72–76.

Urick, M.J. 2014. "The Presentation of Self: Dramaturgical Theory and Generations in Organizations." *Journal of Intergenerational Relationships* 12, no. 4, pp. 398–412.

Urick, M.J., and A. Arslantas. 2018. "A Comparison of US and Turkish Perspectives of Generations." *Gerontology & Geriatrics Studies* 3, no. 1.

Urick, M.J., and E.C. Hollensbe. 2014. "Toward an Identity-Based Perspective of Generations." In *Generational Diversity at Work: New Research Perspectives*, eds. E. Parry, 114–28. New York, NY: Routledge.

Urick, M.J., and V. Crandall. 2012. "Engaging Conflict While Fostering Cooperation – An Organizational Case Study." In *From Identity-Based Conflict to Identity-Based Cooperation: The ARIA Approach in Theory and Practice*, ed. J. Rothman, 157–74. New York, NY: Springer Publications.

Urick, M.J., E.C. Hollensbe, and G.T. Fairhurst. 2017. "Differences in Understanding Generation in the Workforce." *Journal of Intergenerational Relationships* 15, no. 3, pp. 221–40.

Urick, M.J., E.C. Hollensbe, S.S. Masterson, and S.T. Lyons. 2017. "Understanding and Managing Intergenerational Conflict: An Examination of Influences and Strategies." *Work, Aging and Retirement* 3, no. 2, pp. 166–85.

Valentine, S.R., and T.L. Rittenburg. 2007. "Ethical Decision Making of Men and Women Executives in International Business Situations." *Journal of Business Ethics* 71, no. 2, pp. 125–34.

Warhurst, R.P., and K.E. Black. 2015. "It's Never Too Late to Learn." *Journal of Workplace Learning* 27, no. 6, pp. 457–72.

Weber, J. 2015. "Identifying and Assessing Managerial Value Orientations: A Cross-Generational Replication Study of Key Organizational Decision-Makers' Values." *Journal of Business Ethics* 132, no. 3, pp. 493–504.

Weber, J., and M.J. Urick. 2017. "Examining the Millennials' Ethical Profile: Assessing Demographic Variations in Their Personal Value Orientations." *Business and Society Review* 122, no. 4, pp. 469–506.

Wilson, J.A., and N.S. Elman. 1990. "Organizational Benefits of Mentoring." *The Executive* 4, no. 4, pp. 88–94.

Wittgenstein, L. 1953. *Philosophical Investigations.* Oxford: Blackwell.

Zemke, R. 2001. "Here Come the Millennials." *Training* 38, pp. 44–49.

About the Author

Dr. Michael J. Urick is Graduate Director of the Master of Science in Management: Operational Excellence (MSMOE) program and Associate Professor of Management and Operational Excellence at the Alex G. McKenna School of Business, Economics, and Government at St. Vincent College in Latrobe, Pennsylvania. He received his PhD in management (organizational behavior focus) from the University of Cincinnati. His MBA (focused in human resource management) and MS (in leadership and business ethics) are both from Duquesne University in Pittsburgh and his bachelor's degree is from St. Vincent College. In his current role, Dr. Urick teaches undergraduate and graduate courses related to organizational behavior, human resources, communication and conflict, organizational culture, operations, and research methods.

The MSMOE program, which he directs, focuses on providing aspiring leaders with cutting edge management techniques to effectively problem solve, minimize waste, and continuously improve their organizations. The program has been ranked as a "Top 50 Best Value Masters of Management" program by Value Colleges in their two most recent rankings and as a "Top Online Non-MBA Business Graduate Degree" by US News and World Report. Dr. Urick is Six Sigma Green Belt certified and is certified through the Society for Human Resource Management as well as the True Lean program at the University of Kentucky. He is the recipient of an "Excellence in Teaching" award from the Lindner College of Business at the University of Cincinnati as well as the Quentin Schaut Faculty Award from Saint Vincent College. Internationally, Urick was recognized by the Institute for Supply Management as "Person of the Year" in the learning and education category in 2015.

Academically, Urick is an Associate Editor of the *Journal of Leadership and Management* and his research interests include leadership, conflict, and diversity in the workplace. Much of his work focuses on issues related to intergenerational phenomena within organizations. He also often examines how popular culture can be used to advance organizational behavior theory in his research. In addition to dozens of research pieces being published in journals and books, he also regularly presents at academic and practitioner international meetings such as the Academy of Management, Society for Industrial and Organizational Psychology, and Institute for Supply Management conferences. Urick is a regular speaker on age-related issues in the workplace throughout the United States and internationally and is an active consultant on issues related to workplace interactions, organizational culture, and ethics. Michael has served as a reviewer for a variety of academic publications including the *Journal of Intergenerational Relationships, Journal of Social Psychology, Journal of Organizational Behavior*, and *Journal of Family Issues* as well as the Organizational Behavior and Human Resources divisions of the Academy of Management Annual Meeting in addition to other conferences. In his monthly blog on Saint Vincent's website, Urick blends his research and teaching interests to suggest practical and actionable items for readers to use in their current or future work situations.

Professionally, Urick serves on the board of ISM-Pittsburgh and is currently President. Additionally, he volunteers on the board of several other nonprofit organizations. He is also a member of the Society for Human Resource Management. Prior to academia, Urick worked in a variety of roles related to auditing, utilities, environmental issues, and training and development. In these roles, Dr. Urick became fascinated with interactions in the workplace and how they might be improved which has influenced his academic career.

For fun, Urick enjoys music and, since 1998, has led and performed with Neon Swing X-perience, a jazz band that has toured portions of the United States on numerous occasions.

Index

OTHER TITLES IN THE HUMAN RESOURCE MANAGEMENT AND ORGANIZATIONAL BEHAVIOR COLLECTION

- *Conflict First Aid: How to Stop Personality Clashes and Disputes from Damaging You or Your Organization* by Nancy Radford
- *How to Manage Your Career: The Power of Mindset in Fostering Success* by Kelly Swingler
- *Deconstructing Management Maxims, Volume I: A Critical Examination of Conventional Business Wisdom* by Kevin Wayne
- *Deconstructing Management Maxims, Volume II: A Critical Examination of Conventional Business Wisdom* by Kevin Wayne
- *The Real Me: Find and Express Your Authentic Self* by Mark Eyre
- *Across the Spectrum: What Color Are You?* by Stephen Elkins-Jarrett
- *The Human Resource Professional's Guide to Change Management: Practical Tools and Techniques to Enact Meaningful and Lasting Organizational Change* by Melanie J. Peacock
- *Tough Calls: How to Move Beyond Indecision and Good Intentions* by Linda D. Henman
- *The 360 Degree CEO: Generating Profits While Leading and Living with Passion and Principles* by Lorraine A. Moore
- *The Concise Coaching Handbook: How to Coach Yourself and Others to Get Business Results* by Elizabeth Dickinson

Announcing the Business Expert Press Digital Library

Concise e-books business students need for classroom and research

This book can also be purchased in an e-book collection by your library as

- a one-time purchase,
- that is owned forever,
- allows for simultaneous readers,
- has no restrictions on printing, and
- can be downloaded as PDFs from within the library community.

Our digital library collections are a great solution to beat the rising cost of textbooks. E-books can be loaded into their course management systems or onto students' e-book readers.
The **Business Expert Press** digital libraries are very affordable, with no obligation to buy in future years. For more information, please visit **www.businessexpertpress.com/librarians**. To set up a trial in the United States, please email **sales@businessexpertpress.com**.